When God Comes Calling

A journey of faith …
Wall Street to the World

Ted Fletcher

When God Comes Calling
by Ted Fletcher
Copyright ©2001 by PIONEERS

Scriptures marked CEV: From The Holy Bible: The Contemporary English Version, copyright © 1995, American Bible Society

Scriptures marked KJV: From The King James Version

Scriptures marked NIV: From the HOLY BIBLE: New International Version, copyright © 1973, 1978 by the International Bible Society

Scriptures marked NLT: From the Holy Bible, New Living Translation, copyright © 1996. Used by permission of Tyndale House Publishers, Inc., Wheaton, Illinois 60189. All rights reserved.

Scripture marked TMB: From The Message Bible, copyright © 1993 by Eugene H. Peterson; published by NavPress Publishing Group, Colorado Springs, Colorado

Cover design by Bill Johnson, ImageOptions

ISBN 1-58169-070-3
Printed in the U.S.A. For worldwide distribution.

Gazelle Press
An Imprint of Genesis Communications, Inc.
P.O. Box 91011, Mobile, AL 36691
(800) 367-8203

TABLE OF CONTENTS

DEDICATION

To my Lord, who called me into His service.
To my family, who joined me in answering that call.

Ask of me, and I will make the nations your inheritance, the ends of the earth your possession.
—Psalm 2:8 (NIV)

If you can't see very far ahead, go ahead as far as you can see.
—Dawson Trotman

FOREWORD

The God who called Samuel to be a prophet, Paul to be an apostle, and William Carey to innovate an eighteenth-century missionary movement has not lost His voice. He still calls.

God calls some Christians who do not respond. He calls others who respond but do not qualify. He calls still others who qualify but do not complete their task.

Called ones who respond, qualify, and complete God's assignment are a very select company indeed. Ted and Peggy Fletcher—with their founding of PIONEERS—stand in the forefront of that category in our generation. I value every minute that I have been in their presence, every account I have heard of their exploits.

Our minds readily accept God calling a Samuel in a mideastern robe or a Paul in Tarsian sandals. But God calling a Dow Jones executive in a pin-stripe suit boggles us! Ah, Ted and Peggy, how you stretch our limited perceptions of what God can do! Thank you!

—Don Richardson
Author of *Peace Child* and *Eternity in Their Hearts*

With my son, John Fletcher

It has always been my ambition to
preach the gospel where Christ was not known,
so that I would not be building on
someone else's foundation.

ROMANS 15:20 (NIV)

INTRODUCTION

Let us run with perseverance the race marked out for us.
    —Hebrews 12:1 (NIV)

Twenty years from now, you'll be more disappointed by the things you didn't do than the ones you did. So throw off your bowlines. Leave the still waters of the harbor. Catch the trade winds with your sail!
    —Mark Twain

While I was working on this book, tall ships from all over the globe gathered in New York's harbor. It was a spectacular display of vessels from many places around the globe, sailing the waters of one of the most beautiful harbors in the world.

As magnificent as these ships are, however, they're not designed for safe harbors. Ships are designed to sail the open seas.

So it is with pioneers. When God comes calling in our lives, we often have to push our way out of the safe harbor, lose sight of land, and trust Him to lead us to places where we have never been before.

This is the story of what happened when God came calling in the lives of two ordinary people. He called Peggy and me out of a safe harbor, gave us an impossible dream, then provided the grace, people, and resources necessary to bring it to reality. We didn't know how to reach people in far-off lands or how to start a mission agency, but we trusted God to use us.

It is also the story of hundreds of men and women like us, many who had everything the world offered, but weren't content because they wanted what God offered. Andrew Carnegie once said, "I surround myself with people who are smarter than I am, and I let them do their job." That also is the story of PIONEERS—the many talented, gifted, and willing people whom God brings our way. In the few pages of this book, we can't possibly mention the thousands of people who have been so instrumental to PIONEERS in the past two decades. How can we ever thank all our missionaries, prayer partners, supporting churches, donors, board members, and volunteers? Without them, there would be no PIONEERS. Peggy and I are eternally grateful to each one of them.

This is also the story of another pioneer: You. Has God come calling in your life? Is He stirring you to push beyond what is known and comfortable, to explore new regions, to sail out of the safe harbor and into the open seas?

Read this book, and you could find yourself in an Indonesian jungle translating the Bible for an unreached tribe, doing a puppet show on the crowded streets of one of India's mega cities, or quietly sharing your faith over a tiny cup of strong coffee in a marketplace in Morocco.

If you are a pioneer, the way to step toward tomorrow is not to follow, but to lead, to blaze a new path. As we pioneer to reach the unreached, we do it with the strong conviction that there is no place on earth where Christ cannot be proclaimed, and that there is no door too closed that God cannot open. Lost multitudes continue to pass into a Christless eternity. Now is the time to pray, to give, to go. Now is the time to act. Now is the time to pioneer.

Ted Fletcher
Orlando, Florida
July 2001

CHAPTER 1

Licensed to Kill

With your blood you purchased men for God from
every tribe and language and people and nation.
                —Revelation 5:9 (NIV)

When man works, man works; when man prays, God
works.
                —Hudson Taylor

Korea, December 8, 1952
U.S. Marine Corps, Reconnaissance Company
First Division, Patrol #91

Nothing can prepare a person to kill. Or to be killed.

I encountered both that bitter-cold night in Korea half a
century ago. As I trudged across a frozen rice paddy, the tran-
quil meadows and distant mountain peaks contrasted with the
death and misery of war all around me. Just a week earlier, I
had turned twenty-one, but I never felt more alive in my life
than right here in the face of death. That was what I was
trained for. I was Orville Hunt Fletcher, Jr., United States
Marine, #1222744. Man of the night. Licensed to kill.

It was just past 10:00 p.m. Four hours earlier, our platoon of Marines had departed from the combat outpost at Nan 1. We followed a winding stream deep behind enemy lines and were now in the "front yard" of the 65th Chinese People's Liberation Army.

Tonight's mission, for which I had volunteered, was to capture one of their soldiers and take him with us as a prisoner. In a few minutes, we would be in position at the base of a small hill just yards away from the bunker home of thirty Chinese soldiers, which our scouts had spotted just a few days before.

If all went according to plan, the South Korean Marines would attack the Chinese lines from our left flank. When the Chinese soldiers exited their bunker to return fire, Eugene Lenhoff and Kent Nixon, two members of my squad, would seize one of them, gag and bind him, and together we'd take him back for interrogation. As part of the ten-man "snatch squad," I would help to provide covering fire in case we met with resistance. On the dikes behind us were two support teams, and further back, a stretcher squad, which we hoped we wouldn't need. Our test run the night before had gone like clockwork, and we expected the same tonight.

Suddenly, the stillness was sliced by exploding grenades and a sharp volley of shots about forty-five yards to our left rear. Within moments, a fierce fire-fight was underway.

"Majesty, this is Majesty Baker," the radio crackled. "We've made contact with a superior enemy number." It was the voice of Andrew Guidry, radio operator for our support team.

Lieutenant Lee Cook, our platoon leader, ordered us to hold our position and stay down. Fifty yards in front of us, the Chinese were already pouring out of their bunker—fast and furious. They were shooting off flares that lit up the sky as bright as daylight, exposing our position and leaving us no place to hide. We were trapped, and about 700 Chinese soldiers blocked our escape route!

Rudolph Blick and I crouched next to each other, and in a few moments heard a Chinese soldier walking nearby. He spotted us from about thirty feet and called to us in Chinese. When we said nothing, he pulled the pin on a grenade, threw it toward us, and rushed away just as it exploded. Dirt, snow, and ice flew into the air. I looked over at Blick who lay motionless just a foot away from me. I thought he was dead, but he slowly lifted a hand to wipe blood from a wound on his head.

The fierce fighting behind us seemed to die down just a bit when I heard movement and voices coming toward us from where the fighting had been. I glanced at two other members of my squad, who nodded as if to say that they had heard it, too.

Crawling on my stomach, I inched my way closer toward Lieutenant Cook. Another flare illuminated the sky. The snow, adding to the brightness, helped to silhouette the outline of a column of men moving right toward us. They were Chinese soldiers, probably heading back to their bunker. As they drew closer, I could see they were relaxed and engaged in friendly conversation. They obviously had no idea we were right in front of them.

My finger was ready at the trigger of my high-powered semi-automatic rifle. I began to rock restlessly from side to side, waiting for the signal to fire. My senses were fully heightened, and every sight, sound, and even smell were amplified.

"Should I open up?" I whispered to Cook.

"Not yet," he replied, placing a hand on my shoulder.

Each moment seemed to stretch for hours. The enemy

closed in on us, and I could count about twenty soldiers in plain view.

"Should I fire?" I whispered again.

"Not yet." The calmness of Cook's voice failed to reassure me. His hand continued to rest on my shoulder.

Forty feet...thirty...twenty. The Chinese seemed too close now. The dog tags around my neck rubbed against my cold skin as I leaned forward and took aim, waiting for the command to fire.

Suddenly, another flare lit the sky, and I could hardly believe my eyes. The Chinese soldiers were gone! For no apparent reason, they had turned and were heading in the opposite direction! For the moment, they were spared (and we were spared too).

Lieutenant Cook and our radio man made contact with the support squad, and learned our men had suffered casualties. We had to go back to help, but we weren't sure where they were or how to reach them. So as best we could, we followed the directions given to us by radio, slipping and sliding our way across the wide-open rice paddy. My twenty-pound rifle never felt heavier, and at one point I fell hard on the ice, unable to stand up on my own. Two of my fellow Marines helped me to my feet, and we pressed into a hail of bullets.

I wasn't quite prepared for the scene we encountered. Bodies were strewn across the icy field to my right and left, and the white snow was stained with blood—American and Chinese.

Among the more seriously wounded was my buddy Howard Davenport. The Chinese had fired down on him at close range from atop a dike, their bullets tearing into his head, leg, arm, and side. To finish the job, a Chinese soldier dropped a grenade in his face. Miraculously, Davenport was

*My Marine Corps portrait, early 1950s
(with Recon Company insignia)*

With Korean orphan

still alive, although the grenade's detonation jolted his eyeballs from their sockets.

One of our squad, George Samaha, told Davenport to stay low while he fired a base of gunfire to repel the Chinese who were trying to capture him. Rolling onto his back, Davenport kicked off a wounded Chinese soldier and did his best to crawl on his back in the direction of Samaha's voice.

Lloyd Smalley, also from our squad, began crawling toward Davenport, and grasping his hand, dragged him across the frozen ground. Just as they reached a cut in the rice paddy, a bullet pierced Smalley's throat. He saved Davenport, but it cost him his own life.

We were still drawing heavy fire and fighting for our lives. "Lord, help us," I prayed as I opened up on the enemy with my rifle.

At last, the Chinese abandoned their position and hastily withdrew. As our stretcher squad moved in to tend to the wounded, I helped others police the area, looking for weapons and searching the dead Chinese. One Chinese soldier was lying face down, and I turned him over and found myself looking into the eyes of a young teenager, probably fourteen or fifteen years old. His body was still warm. I pulled open his clothes to look for documents that might tell us something about his comrades in arms.

We had inflicted a heavy toll upon the enemy: Seven killed, another four whom we believed were killed and removed, and eleven wounded.

An evacuation team covered our withdrawal back to Nan 1, where we arrived a little after midnight. Trucks took us back to our company base, and just before sun-up I finally got to my tent—bone-tired yet deep in thought. On earlier patrols, I had heard and smelled the enemy, but this was my first fire-fight. I was thankful to be alive and knew it was only because God had miraculously answered my prayer to help us in this impossible situation.

That night, and over the next two weeks, I wrestled with questions that plagued my soul—profound, deep questions that I couldn't answer, yet couldn't escape.

Yes, I was prepared to kill—trained and licensed to do so. But was I prepared to die?

One icy morning two weeks later, everyone was talking about a young American preacher who was visiting the troops in Korea. Just four years earlier, this fiery evangelist from North Carolina had leapt onto the front pages of American newspapers during his famous tent crusade in Los Angeles.

His name was Billy Graham, and he was scheduled to hold a meeting later that day at our division headquarters. The meeting was open to anyone who wanted to attend. As I thought about the opportunity, I remembered something my dad once told me. "Son, if you ever get the chance to hear Billy Graham preach, don't miss it." Today was my chance.

I grabbed my bullet-proof New Testament, a gift from my sister Martha, and recruited three others from Recon Company to go with me. We boarded a truck for division headquarters and walked across the frozen compound to a bowl-shaped, natural amphitheatre at the base of the hills surrounding Marine headquarters.

I took a seat on one of the sandbags facing a platform that had been hastily constructed the day before. One of the men had painted a large picture of Jesus watching over a Marine, which he and his friends had brought by jeep, under cover of darkness, from their front-line trench almost forty miles away.

Before long, a convoy of jeeps arrived, with the commanding general of our division and almost his entire staff escorting our guest. After a brief introduction, Rev. Graham stood to speak. He explained that he was on the final stretch of an eleven-day visit to Korea, yet today was the only time he would address the Marines on the front lines.

Rev. Graham told us that he had come to Korea with Good News—the Good News of the Gospel of Jesus Christ. But at first, it didn't sound so good. He said that our sins had separated us from a holy God and that there was a penalty for our sin: death. We would all die someday—whether in battle as young men or later in life—and then would have to face the consequences for our sin. As he spoke, I felt as if I'd peered into the flames of hell itself and faced myself as a lost, sinful man.

Then Rev. Graham gave us the Good News with such clarity and simplicity that even a child could have understood. He quoted John 3:16 from the Bible: "For God so loved the world, that he gave his only begotten Son, that whosoever believeth in him should not perish, but have everlasting life" (KJV).

With burning intensity, his eyes searched the crowd as he asked us if we were ready to meet God. He seemed to be looking at and talking directly to me. Up to this point in my life, I had considered myself a Christian. Growing up, I attended Baptist, Methodist, Presbyterian, and Episcopal churches, prayed whenever I needed to, and lived a good life. None of that seemed to matter now. I knew I was not ready to meet my Creator. I was lost and in need of salvation, and none of my good works could earn it for me.

Rev. Graham explained that the greatest battle of my life was being waged right then and there. He made it clear: There was no in-between ground. He said we were enemies of God because of our sin, and we had to surrender to His claim upon our lives. "Will you surrender your life to Jesus Christ?" he asked us. "Will you ask Him to save you from your sins and receive the free gift of salvation that He offers to you?"

Billy Graham shares the Gospel with Marines at front during Korean War as I listen (see circle).

Photos courtesy of the Billy Graham Center

Fletcher family 1945 (Back row, left to right: Ted, Waller, Martha. Middle row: Bill, Orville Hunt Fletcher, Sr. [father], Virginia Elizabeth Fletcher [mother], Mary Jane. Front row: John and Harry)

Surrender. For a moment, I wondered if Rev. Graham had chosen the wrong word. How could his message ever persuade a group of battle-hardened Marines who would rather die fighting than surrender? Yet, I knew that how I responded to this invitation would not only determine my eternal destiny, but also make a difference for the rest of my life here on earth.

"If you will accept Christ today," he continued, "I want you to make your decision public and stand up." Without hesitation, I made my choice and stood to surrender to Jesus Christ. Several hundred men did the same, including my three fellow Recon Company Marines and our commander, Major General Edwin A. Pollack. As Rev. Graham led us in a prayer, words that I thought I could never say fell naturally from my lips.

> Lord Jesus, I surrender my life to You. I believe that You died on the cross of Calvary in my place to pay the penalty for my sin. I believe that You rose again. Please come into my life. I receive You as my personal Savior and Lord.

The date was December 23, 1952, and although the Korean War continued for another seven months, the battle for the soul of Ted Fletcher was over. Jesus Christ had won.

When Rev. Graham returned to the U.S., he wrote his reflections of that cold Korean morning:

> I will never forget that first meeting at the front. Many of these men had been on patrol duty the night before...many had traveled on foot from their trenches and bunkers to attend the service.... Everyone had his rifle and was in full fighting gear. They were extremely responsive and interested in the message. Not once did I use any humor or any emo-

tional stories. There was no need. These men were ready for the Word of God.

When I gave the invitation, more than one-third of the men stood to their feet in front of their buddies to accept Jesus Christ as Savior. Many were weeping unashamedly, men who had faced death just hours before; big, strong, tough Marines, weeping because of their sins and their need of a Savior.

Never in my ministry have I preached with more liberty or power. The Spirit of God seemed to fall on that meeting.[1]

In the weeks that followed, I was like a sponge soaking up all the vital truths of the faith. I enrolled in a Navigators' Scripture memory course and learned to love the Bible. I began to realize that my life actually belonged to Jesus Christ. God placed on my heart a desire to tell others about His Son, and so I did, wherever I went and to anyone who would listen. There and then, I wanted my faith to be filled with adventure and passion.

I also began to understand that God had given me a new mission in life—to love the world with the same love that He had shown to me. No longer was I merely a man of the night trained to kill. I was now Ted Fletcher, child of God, licensed to serve the living God.

CHAPTER 2

Ordinary Son

The time has now come to bring together the people
of every language and nation and to show them my
glory.
                    —Isaiah 66:18 (CEV)

If you want to succeed, you should strike out on new
paths rather than travel the worn paths of accepted
success.
                    —John D. Rockefeller, Jr.

Herman Washington Fletcher breathed deeply as he tied
another log to his mule. One more log would yield him a few
more sawn planks, and soon the house he was building for his
bride, Calla, would be complete. His timing was none too
soon, because the crops in the field were almost ripe, and
every available hand was needed to bring in the harvest.

The Fletcher family has roots deep in the soil of that farm
in Boxville, Kentucky. My great-grandfather, George Parker
Hunt, purchased the acreage in 1855, and when he died of
pneumonia at the age of thirty-five, his wife was left with four
children and a mortgage. A schoolteacher, she somehow paid
off the mortgage before she, too, died; typhoid fever claimed
her at age forty-two. Various relatives took in her children, in-

cluding Calla, who went to Illinois to be raised by her cousin. When Calla came of age, she moved back to Kentucky and took control of the family farm, marrying Herman Fletcher when she was just nineteen. Their first child arrived on November 7, 1904—Orville Hunt Fletcher, my father. They named him after Orville Wright, the pioneer of aviation whose historic first flight had made headlines just a year earlier.

Farm life at the turn of the twentieth century was demanding. Electricity was still many years away, and water for cooking, drinking, and washing was carried in a bucket from the well in front of the house. Grandma made her own soap, washed clothes on a scrub-board, and sewed with a foot-treadle sewing machine. Grandpa milked the cows, fed the pigs, and plowed the fields. When Dad wasn't in school, he would be right by Grandpa's side. In the evenings, neighbors would gather on Grandpa's porch with their guitars, banjos, mandolins, and fiddles—and the night would come alive with wonderful bluegrass music.

Dad was an avid sportsman in high school, and especially good at baseball. By the time he graduated, the St. Louis Cardinals and Boston Braves were knocking on his door. Those offers must have been tempting, but he followed the advice of his coach and turned them all down to enter the University of Kentucky at Lexington.

One day, a young coed on campus, Virginia Davis, caught his attention. Dad won her affections, and they were married on October 18, 1926.

Mom had grown up in a home where her mother taught that the Bible and faith were the strong foundations of family life. Her great-grandfather was a Baptist preacher for more than fifty years, and "Old Pappy" would regularly get his grandchildren and great-grandchildren on their knees praying. He was 101 years old when he died.

As in all marriages, Mom and Dad started out their new life together full of promise, but as the Great Depression deepened, they were forced to drop out of school to make ends meet. One day with nowhere else to turn, Dad cried out to the Lord for help. He felt his burden lift, and not long after, his Uncle Waller arrived with a gift of new shoes, some money, and a lead on a job at a high school—teaching history and coaching football, basketball, and baseball.

Their family quickly grew—first Waller, then Martha, and finally I arrived on December 1, 1931. My parents named me after Dad, the greatest honor of my life. Over the next decade, other children followed—Mary Jane, Bill, John, and Harry.

Raising a family during the Great Depression was no easy matter, yet Dad managed to return to the University of Kentucky to complete his degree while Mom cared for us on the family farm. When Dad graduated in 1932, he joined more than 12 million Americans who were unemployed and looking for work. With those grim numbers, it didn't matter that he had a degree in hand; he took what he was offered—a job with the B&O Railroad in Dayton, Ohio, first as a brakeman, and later as yard master working twelve-hour shifts, seven days a week.

Sometimes, Dad would let me go to work with him. I knew he must be someone important because everyone called him "Doc." I learned later that was because he dressed in a suit and tie and looked like a doctor! While Dad conducted his business, I would sit in his office and draw, write, or play on his typewriter. Occasionally, I'd wander across the street and buy some candy from a store where John Dillinger, one of America's most notorious criminals, used to hang out not many years before.

Dad worked long hours, eventually becoming a division superintendent, yet he never let his position keep him from befriending or helping railroad laborers. Today we would call him a servant-leader. At the time I wasn't aware of the many sleepless nights he put in; all I saw was that he autographed his work with excellence.

Mom made sure we all knew the meaning of hard work, too. Many a Saturday morning began with the words I came to dread: "Today is the workiest of work days!" she would cheerfully announce. All my friends were sleeping in, but not the Fletchers. Mom had our full attention and a long list of chores to get done around the house. We maintained a healthy respect for our parents' authority. Dad could be a stern disciplinarian, and Mom's strong hand kept us in line when he was away. There were very few times when they told us a second time to do something.

Mom ran the house like Dad ran the railroad—on time and within budget. She knew how to stretch a dollar further than anyone I knew. One year she decided to raise chickens to eat. Then she took up photography and set up a studio and darkroom in our house. No matter who stopped by—relative, friend, or insurance salesman—they had to pose for a picture. She later added antiques to her list of hobbies—collecting and selling them. When Waller and I launched a basement cleaning business, she had first claim on whatever junk we hauled from the homes of our "clients," who never knew how Mom turned their trash into treasure.

Mom liked to make money, but she liked giving it away even more. Her greatest gift was that she gave of herself to her family. She knew I had a hunger for adventure that was unbounded. When I was young, she took me on a train ride to Chicago, where we shopped at Marshall Fields, ate at Coopers Cafeteria, and even dipped our hands into Lake Michigan.

Mom loved without holding tightly and gave me a long leash. By the time I was twelve years old, I was hitchhiking all

over Indiana and Ohio with my friend Maynard Clark. Big
freight trucks would pick us up, then drop us off to explore
new places. When I was sixteen and living in Indiana, a friend
and I hitchhiked our way down to Texas, and when Grandma
Fletcher was dying in a Kentucky hospital in 1948, I hitchhiked to see her before she passed away.

Mom made me feel that with God's help I could do anything, no matter what the obstacles. "You can do it!" she'd
encourage me. With Mom, there was always a way. All I
needed to do was to find it.

We would often take vacations back at the Fletcher family
farm in Kentucky. Grandpa would let us ride the horses, and
Grandma would fill us up with biscuits and chicken gravy. On
Sundays and for revival services, we'd head to the little one-
room country church. Grandma was raised in the Christian
Church and had a genuine love for the Scriptures, especially
the writings of Paul. Whenever we were around the house, I'd
hear her singing songs like "Jesus Loves Me," "The Old
Rugged Cross," "Rock of Ages," and other hymns.

She must have instilled that faith in her son because Dad
was a deeply spiritual man and the spiritual leader in our
home. His favorite book was the Bible, and he honored and
revered it as the sacred Word of God, regularly reading it
aloud to us. He believed in God's absolute power, including
the power to heal.

One afternoon when my younger brother Bill was
working at a local farm, he fell off a culti-packer with a big
iron disk that ran right over him. Unconscious and lying in a
pool of blood, he looked as if half his head had been cut off.
In fact, his scalp was just barely attached, and the back of his
head was completely exposed. An ambulance raced him to the
hospital, where Dad boldly got down on his knees in the
lobby and begged God to spare the life of his son. God an-

swered his prayer, and after months in the hospital and at home recovering from the surgery, Bill had only a scar to remind him of God's mercy.

I also learned about the Lord from one of our neighbors, Helen Salisbury, who had led my sister Martha to the Lord. Mrs. Salisbury invited me to attend the "Miracle Book Club" that she hosted in her home. She read us Bible stories, and told us we needed to make a personal decision of faith in Jesus Christ for salvation. I wasn't sure what it all meant, but one day I raised my hand and went through the motions of asking Jesus into my heart.

When the world turned to war in the 1940s, Dad hung a large map on the wall, where he'd plot the movements of the Allied forces. He kept up on current events and would captivate us with stories about battles happening in far-off places all over the world.

Mom and Dad put an emphasis on education, but I have to admit that I loved sports more than my studies. By the time I was in high school in Garrett, Indiana, I was playing first-string halfback on the varsity football team, the "Mighty Railroaders," and starred on the track team, running the 440-yard dash and the mile relay. During the summer, I joined the rest of the town working on the railroad.

While we were growing up, it seemed as if we moved as often as the trains did. Every time Dad was promoted, we sold our old house, packed up everything we owned, and started life all over again in a new community with new friends and schools. The constant moves made us appreciate each other and knit us into a close family. From Indiana, we moved to Pittsburgh, Pennsylvania. I graduated from Mount Lebanon High School in 1950, and attended the University of Indiana at Bloomington where my older brother, Waller, was already enrolled.

In ordinary times, I would have looked forward to four years as an undergraduate—but these were not ordinary times. Just a few months earlier, the North Korean army had invaded South Korea. America feared that Communism, which was already entrenched in Russia and China, might gain yet another foothold and eventually engulf all of Asia. President Harry S. Truman ordered U.S. ground forces to Korea, and fifteen other nations joined the Americans under the umbrella of the United Nations Command. At home, however, the pursuit of prosperity and the good life filled the soul of a nation that had endured years of depression, followed by years of war in Europe and the Pacific. No one wanted another war, and newspapers were not carrying much news about what was happening half a world away.

As I settled into classes at the university, the war in Korea moved into full swing, and everywhere I looked there were Armed Forces recruiting posters. One in particular had special appeal to me. It was a picture of a battle-hardened Marine and read, "We don't promise you a rose garden! United States Marine Corps." Another had a picture of Uncle Sam pointing his finger, with the words, "We don't want you! We want men! United States Marine Corps."

Able-bodied men were needed to expel the communists from Korea and stem the flow of Communism into the free world. I sensed history in the making! *Should I seize the moment and enlist?* I asked myself. *I could always complete my education later,* I reasoned. *Besides, all my life I had wanted to be a Marine.* I admired the aggressive toughness and can-do spirit of America's oldest military service, not to mention its ability to quickly deploy troops to far-flung crisis areas.

Finally, I made my decision. Even though truce talks had already begun, I walked into a recruiting office in Cincinnati, Ohio, on August 22, 1951, and enlisted. The next day, the communists broke off the peace talks, and I headed to boot camp.

My introduction to Parris Island, South Carolina, was everything I had heard and worse. From the moment our bus arrived, the drill instructors (DIs) did everything they could to intimidate us—yelling, cursing, and threatening us every waking moment. They were brutal dictators, and we were at their mercy. We were a bunch of wanna-be Marines who didn't know the first thing about war. Our DIs had their work cut out for them.

The physical side of our training was demanding. We endured a grueling obstacle course and never-ending repetitions of every exercise known to man. Every day we marched, crisscrossing the grounds, back and forth. In the heat of the day, a flag would sometimes be raised, indicating that the temperature was higher than acceptable health standards. Our DIs could not have cared less. Instead, they would march us behind the barracks, out of sight of their superiors.

The high stress, hazing, and rough treatment that we endured was designed to develop respect for authority, physical stamina, and mental fortitude. DIs had a way of solving disciplinary problems right on the spot with a kick in the pants, a fist in the stomach, fifty push-ups, endless marching, or worse.

Although Parris Island had all the charm of a maximum-security prison, three months of demanding, backbreaking training transformed a ragtag class of recruits into a new generation of gritty, gung-ho "leathernecks." The Marine Corps' motto, "Semper Fidelis" (Always Faithful), was inscribed on our hearts. We were taught to watch each other's backs, and that we had an obligation and accountability to our fellow Marines. We also learned an important lesson: to accomplish a hard mission, we had to push ourselves to the limit, then beyond—and never, ever give up.

Graduation Day finally arrived, and I was proud to have

survived the toughest school on earth. I was now one of "The few. The proud. The Marines."

Next stop was Camp Lejeune in Jacksonville, North Carolina, where I learned more about the legendary Reconnaissance (Recon) Company, an elite Marine Corps service battalion. The Company's motto—"Swift, Silent, Deadly"—and special mystique intrigued me, and the thought of being on a cloak-and-dagger mission behind enemy lines seemed especially exciting. When the opportunity came, I volunteered and was accepted.

Preparing for war was tough. In the months that followed, I underwent special training for amphibious reconnaissance. Simulated missions were as real as they could make them, even involving rubber boats launched from submarines. We practiced our maneuvers over and over again until they were second nature, and we learned to "flourish under conditions of uncertainty." Since Recon Company Marines go to war in small units, our instructors drilled into us the concept of teamwork. With teamwork, we would live; without it, we would die.

Over time, we all felt that our Recon Company was "the best of the best," and that we could face any danger and take on any challenge to get the job done. As the "eyes and ears" of the division, our Recon Company trained for a variety of missions that would keep our troops abreast of the Chinese: surveillance (probing behind enemy lines to collect information on troop concentrations and movements), terrain reconnaissance (checking roads, bridges, and other sites), and intelligence (gathering information by staging an ambush and capturing prisoners).

By the end of the summer of 1952, I had been in training for a year and was tired of war games. All my requests to go overseas for the real thing kept coming back denied; others were "waiting in line" in front of me. In Korea, the truce talks were deadlocked, and I prayed that God would let me go before the war was over. As a final act of desperation, I wrote letters to Senator Robert Taft of Ohio and Senator Earl Clements of Kentucky, a childhood friend of my father's. I stated my plight and asked them to intervene, if possible, on my behalf. To this day, I don't know if one of them actually did intervene, but within a few weeks, my orders arrived. I was on my way to the Western Front in Korea to fight with the First Marine Division.

First, however, was a ten-day furlough. It was great to see my family again, although it was a solemn time for all of us. The night before I left, Mom prepared a farewell dinner, and as we gathered around the table, Dad said an eloquent and moving prayer, asking God to protect me and give me good success in battle.

Boarding a U.S. Navy ship with several thousand other battle-ready young men, I was enveloped with a sense of honor and anticipation. For the first time in my life, I was leaving the shores of my homeland. Destiny was in the wind. I was on a mission—to fight as a United States Marine! Although we were well trained, we were untested, and, privately, many of us on board that ship wondered how we would perform under enemy fire. The camaraderie of a close-knit unit that was trained for dangerous missions is hard to describe. We all knew we needed one another, and that any laxity or failure to follow a particular plan to the letter might cost a life—our own or a buddy's. We were a unique fraternity, the sons of America's families, friends and brothers in battle. We were men of the night who lived in the shadow of death.

At first, my itch for combat led me to volunteer for every mission, regardless of its danger, but after a series of deadly encounters, I decided to be a bit more selective—at least when I had the choice.

A few weeks after Billy Graham came to the front, our Recon Company was part of a strategy that became known as one of the showpiece combat missions in the latter half of the Korean War. We were at full strength that day; anyone who could walk, even the cooks and bottle washers, joined us. In broad daylight, we descended a hill in full view of the enemy. By design, we offered ourselves up as a decoy to make the Chinese reveal themselves. They must have thought that the entire First Marine Division was about to push forward in a major offensive because they quickly reinforced their positions on the hills. Then our tanks fired smoke-screen shells into the "no-man's land" between the Chinese and us.

As the enemy responded with mortar fire, our Marine Air Wing came in with low-flying assault planes, strafing the Chinese lines and launching a brutal napalm attack. The utter mayhem of war was horrific beyond words.

This is the end, I thought. The pounding was relentless, continuing for hours, and I couldn't see how we would ever make it out alive. I repeated the only Scripture that I could re-member—the Twenty-Third Psalm: "The Lord is my shep-herd; I shall not want. He maketh me to lie down in green pastures; he leadeth me beside the still waters" (verses 1-2, KJV).

As I lay on my back, once again I faced the fact of my own mortality—yet this time with the full assurance that I was ready to meet God. Over and over again, I repeated the words, "Though I walk through the valley of the shadow of death, I will fear no evil" (verse 4 KJV)—the primal cry of my soul reassuring itself of God's protection for a desperate time like this. Eventually the fighting ended, and once more I had passed safely through the shadow of death.

Within a four-month period, our company of 120 Marines sustained a casualty rate of approximately seventy percent. I mentioned none of this in my letters home, so as not to alarm my family. Instead, I would give the impression that I was stuck in headquarters, a safe distance from the front lines. Dad suspected otherwise, and he would often feel a burden to pray for me, wondering if at that moment I was in peril. Mom set aside every Friday as a day of fasting and prayer for my safety.

Even my brother, Waller, although not a Christian at the time, told me that he had prayed for me on his birthday— January 28, 1953. I remember that particular night well because we were on patrol when all of a sudden the Chinese ambushed us. Our point man, Kent Nixon, was wounded severely in the stomach, but we all made it out alive—grateful that the trigger-happy Chinese had failed to wait for us to completely pass through their ambush.

There were many other times that I saw God's hand of protection on my own life and those of my fellow Marines. Whether it was an unexplained delay at a crucial moment, or supernatural courage in the face of overwhelming odds, I am forever grateful that I began the war by turning over control of my life to the Lord Jesus.

Finally, after two years of truce talks, a cease-fire went into effect at 10:00 p.m. on July 27, 1953. Two nations, drenched with the spilled blood of seventeen other nations, were left to heal and pick up the pieces. Mao proclaimed the war "a great victory" for the communists, but at what an awful price—4 million Koreans (military and civilians) and 1 million Chinese military gave their lives.

Thirty-seven brutal months had also taken a terrible toll on the U.S, making it one of the costliest wars in our history. More than 1.5 million Americans served in Korea; 36,940 were killed, 103,284 were wounded, and 5,178 were missing or captured.

A month after the cease-fire went into effect, I was released from active duty. Tired of seeing people maimed and killed, I was ready for home. They say, "War is hell on earth," and in some ways I'd have to agree. It's also true that a Marine never fully comes home after a war. Historians later referred to the Korean War as "the Forgotten War," but it would never be that to me. How could I ever forget? For years to come, the haunting memories of battle would awaken me in the middle of the night. Mysteriously, half a century later, I still weep at the thought of certain people or experiences from my time in Korea. I guess that's one reason why within our ranks we say, "Once a Marine, always a Marine."

My journey to the precipice of death forced me to grow up in many ways. In fact, it seemed a lifetime had passed during my nine months and two days overseas. I was a changed man—a new man, bound for Heaven and in search of a new path for my life.

CHAPTER 3

Coming Home

Whether you turn to the right or to the left, your ears
will hear a voice behind you, saying, "This is the way;
walk in it."

—Isaiah 30:21 (NIV)

God provides the wind, but man must raise the sails.
—Saint Augustine

"My son! My son's home!" Dad called out. He was
watching for me from the window, and spotted me as I walked
up the driveway of our house at 222 Bower Hill Road in
Pittsburgh, Pennsylvania. The entire family gathered at the
door to welcome me home. What a joy to be together again! I
enjoyed the luxury of Mom's home cooking—the first real
food I'd had in almost two years—and catching up on the
latest family news.

America itself seemed new, and the options for my own
future were endless. Happily, there was still time to register for
the fall semester at the University of Indiana. My brother,
Waller, who had been so much fun to be with in 1951, had
graduated and I was on my own. I had no problem fitting
back in, but campus life had lost its sparkle. And even though
the GI Bill covered my tuition, finances were still tight.

The thought of moving home to attend the University of Pittsburgh seemed like the best alternative. Dad said that while he couldn't help me much financially, I was certainly welcome to live at home. The decision was not a hard one. I enrolled in business administration at "Pitt" for the spring semester of 1954. The following year, in addition to a full load of evening classes, I added a full-time job as an officer in the real estate department of Fidelity Trust Company. On Sundays, I attended the United Presbyterian Church with my family.

It was a busy schedule, yet compared to war, student life in middle America in the 1950s seemed bland and mundane to me. Inwardly, I was longing for something...or was it someone?

One summer day, just before I started my senior year, my brother-in-law's sister, Lois, was visiting our house, and half jokingly I said to her, "I want to meet a redhead. Do you know any?" I have no idea why I made such a bold request of someone I hardly knew. Yet to my surprise, Lois said she had just the girl for me—an attractive, vivacious redhead who lived across town, a twenty-two-year-old schoolteacher named Peggy Close.

The only problem was that Peggy already had a boyfriend. Lois was persuasive, however, and Peggy agreed to join me at a popular local spot. Tucked into a small booth, we talked the evening away. Peggy fascinated me, and we seemed to have a lot in common. She also had attended Pitt and had just graduated with her B.S. degree in education.

We walked together outside in the warm summer evening, and I decided to ask Peggy a question that at the time was radical: "If you died tonight, how would you know if you'd go to Heaven?"

To Peggy, a faithful member of the First Presbyterian

Church in Wilkinsburg, the question seemed strangely direct. "If my good deeds outweigh my bad deeds, then I'll go to Heaven," she replied matter-of-factly. As we walked, I shared my experience of how I had come to know Christ personally. Peggy was impressed that I could actually quote Bible verses and that I talked about prayer as if it were more than just a ritual. Most of all, she was struck with the assurance that I had from God about my personal salvation.

Before we parted, I asked Peggy to go out with me again the following night. She politely declined, telling me that she already had a date. When I suggested that she just cancel it, she mumbled something about owing him more than that. Somehow, though, I went home that night with an exciting sense that Peggy would become an important part of my future.

The next morning, Peggy phoned her girlfriend Barbara Bruckman and said, "I'm going to marry Ted Fletcher someday." That night, she informed her boyfriend, Chip Harner, that their relationship was over. It would be a while before I knew the private longing that Peggy had carried for years—to marry a Christian man who would help to establish a Christian home.

Peggy's invitation that I join her family for a Labor Day picnic that Monday caught me by surprise. I readily accepted, of course, and was introduced to the Close family: her parents, Malcolm and Frances; her sister, Dorothea, who was twelve years older than Peggy, and her brother Tom, who had fought in General Patton's army in World War II. I later met Peggy's other brother, Bobby, who was a colonel in the Army and had also served with Patton.

Peggy's father had dropped out of school after the third grade, yet became manager of industrial relations (what we would call human resources today) at Mine Safety Appliance

Company in Pittsburgh. His engaging personality and love for people made him a popular and much-loved man among the company's 3,000 employees. Everyone knew "Red" Close. Her mother was a warm-hearted, kind woman, whose life was wrapped up in family and home responsibilities.

Despite the fact that her parents were not church-goers, Peggy was baptized in the local Presbyterian church not long after birth. On Sundays, her Mom would dress the children and send them off to church. Eventually, the kids started attending a Methodist church where the minister spoke about the need for a personal experience of salvation.

Her aunts, Margaret and Edna Close, influenced her greatly. A special bond existed between these two sisters—unmarried schoolteachers who lived together and attended church together. To Peggy, their devotion to God seemed unusual; they not only read their Bibles faithfully, but they even got on their knees to pray!

One day during Peggy's elementary school years, her aunts introduced her to a missionary friend, Eva Harding, who was home on furlough from India. Her silk sari and exotic tales from a far-off land enthralled Peggy. Peggy met Miss Harding a number of times while she was growing up. On the last occasion, the elderly missionary said she was returning to India and might never come back to America again. *What commitment,* Peggy thought, and began dreaming about the possibility of some day becoming a missionary herself.

When the Close family moved to another part of Pittsburgh, Peggy joined her new friends at the local Presbyterian church, and by the time she reached high school, most of her free time was swallowed up in church activities and weekly youth meetings. A yearly highlight was the Westminster Fellowship Youth Conference, held each summer at Grove City College. There, Peggy renewed her devotion to God at campfire dedication services.

*Wedding day,
March 1, 1956*

*Peggy Close,
high school graduation,
1951*

With our children in 1964: Ginny, John, Arlene, and Carol

During her senior year in high school, Peggy began dating Wayne McCoy. Single and in his first year at seminary, Wayne was the new associate pastor at the other Presbyterian church in town. Wayne encouraged Peggy spiritually, and in the fall of 1951, she enrolled in the College of Wooster, a prestigious Presbyterian school in Wooster, Ohio, to pursue a major in religious education. A year later, she transferred to the University of Pittsburgh to major in education. The Heinz Chapel, a landmark on campus that symbolized the spiritual roots of the university, was home to a well-known choir of fifty of the finest voices on campus. Peggy had a beautiful voice and loved music, so she auditioned and was invited to join the renowned group.

Sundays soon became her busiest day of the week. In the mornings, she would sing around the city in churches that needed vocalists to supplement their own choirs. The five dollars she received helped to cover her weekly streetcar commute to and from school. Later in the day, the Heinz Chapel Choir sang sacred music at the KDKA-TV studio, which was televised on the local station in Pittsburgh. Peggy also sang at the Choir's afternoon service at Heinz Chapel, and during spring break she joined the Choir on tour throughout the eastern U.S.

She also joined the Delta Zeta sorority, which at the University of Pittsburgh was noted for its scholastic achievement. Outgoing and popular, Peggy kept a full social calendar. When I met her a few months after graduation, I was convinced the Lord had been saving her just for me.

I remember how excited I was to take Peggy home to meet my parents for the first time. Mom had already gone to bed by the time we arrived, but she came downstairs to meet the young woman she had been hearing so much about. Mom and Dad both loved Peggy and treated her as a daughter from that day forward.

Over the next few months, we dated regularly. I never seemed to mind the forty-five minute drive across town from my house to hers. Increasingly, I knew that Peggy was the one with whom I wanted to spend the rest of my life.

On Christmas Eve, I gave Peggy a diamond ring, and two months later, on March 1, 1956, we were married at the United Presbyterian Church in Mount Lebanon. We honeymooned (on borrowed cash from my sister Martha) at a little resort hotel in Somerset, Pennsylvania, just off the Pennsylvania Turnpike.

Since Peggy was on spring break from her first teaching assignment, we hurried back to settle into our efficiency apartment at Amberson Gardens. Life seemed grand in those days, and I knew first-hand the truth of Proverbs 18:22: "A man's greatest treasure is his wife—she is a gift from the Lord" (CEV).

CHAPTER 4

The Corporate Climb

A man plans his course, but the Lord determines his steps.
—Proverbs 16:9 (NIV)

The world we live in does not offer any lasting security. It can't. What it does offer is trials, challenges, and a whole lot of opportunity. Our security can only be found in our obedience to God's call on our lives.
—John Maxwell

A million dollars! I had never seen so many zeroes. And my name was on the check—not as the payee, unfortunately, but as one of the co-signers at Fidelity Trust, where I worked. The check was for Gulf Oil Company, one of our clients, who maintained an account under a dummy corporation called Tremarco. Word eventually leaked out that the money would help fuel the oil company's billion-dollar expansion program. One of my associates, who was much older and wiser than I, said, "Fletcher, buy as much Gulf stock as you can get your hands on! Oil companies are 'hot.' If you can ever land a job with one, take it."

His stock advice went in one ear and out the other. I had

little money to buy much of anything in those days, but a job with an oil company was within the realm of possibility. I kept my eyes open, and it wasn't long before I found what I was looking for.

On October 23, 1956, I was interviewed for a position as a sales representative with Mobil Oil Corporation. I remember the exact date because of something even more significant that happened the very same day: Peggy gave birth to our first child, Virginia Elizabeth, named after my mother. We called her Ginny, and I wanted everyone I met to know I had a beautiful little girl.

Between a new baby and a new job, life was certainly exciting. At twenty-four years old, I was a father—and employed by a national icon, the same company that had lubricated America's first automobile, the Wright Brothers' first airplane, and Charles Lindbergh's "Spirit of St. Louis." And this same "black gold" or "Texas Tea" was fueling America's ascent into a season of unparalleled affluence and economic growth.

When my training period at Mobil was complete, the company gave me responsibility for my own stations. My employer, Bill Hurst, was demanding and knew how to motivate his sales force. After a year, division management asked Mr. Hurst to recommend someone for a new promotional program being launched in Richmond, Virginia. He gave them my name, and they appointed me, so Peggy and I packed our bags and were on our way.

Richmond was a tough market for Mobil. Not only were our stations small, but our main competitor, Esso (now Exxon), held a twenty-five percent share of the market. My first challenge as an area sales representative was to recruit, train, and promote qualified independent dealers to lease and operate Mobil-owned stations.

As the business grew, so did the amount of time I spent

on the road visiting the stations in my area. Peggy proved to be the perfect mate, supportive of what I was doing. At the time, our country was caught up in the post-war era of abundance and prosperity. Yet, there was an increasing restlessness inside me. I remembered the Billy Graham meeting in Korea where I first heard the Good News that God offered salvation to everyone through His Son, Jesus Christ. Ever since then, I freely shared about the Lord with my friends, business associates, and people I came in contact with. I thought everyone should have at least one opportunity to know about the Lord and how to get to Heaven.

One Sunday morning shortly after we moved to Richmond, Peggy and I attended a service at our church, Bon Air Baptist. The speaker was the candidate secretary for the Southern Baptist International Mission Board and was in charge of recruiting missionaries. He had just returned from India and shared staggering statistics of how there were only a few missionaries for the multitude of Hindu people. It bothered me that Hindus in India, and other people around the world, could live their entire lives and then die without ever meeting a Christian or hearing the Gospel.

I made an appointment to meet with him at the mission board's headquarters in Richmond, and I shared my testimony and heart with him. In essence, I was exploring what it would take for Peggy and me to become missionaries.

I was dismayed when he said that prospective missionaries needed three years of seminary training in order to qualify, and I left confused and without a clear sense of direction. People were living in far-off lands without the Gospel, and it wasn't very easy for a young Christian like me to get involved in reaching them.

Our involvement at church continued. During the week, I taught a church Bible study at the home of our neighbor,

Lucille Scott. One day I shared with her that I wanted to be in a church that was more focused on reaching the lost. Mrs. Scott said she had been feeling the same hunger and said she knew just the church—Immanuel Baptist, an independent congregation not far from our neighborhood.

Peggy and I made plans to visit at an evening service. The pastor, Richard Sueme, wasn't there that night, but it didn't matter. I knew right away that this was the church for us. On one wall was an enormous world map with lights pinpointing different countries where missionaries worked to spread the Gospel—missionaries that this church supported. There were even prayer cards with names and photos of each missionary. I got the feeling that missions wasn't just a once-a-year event for this church; it was the entire focus of the church, 365 days a year.

On September 9, 1958, God blessed us with a son, John, and we saw the Lord moving in his life from a very early age. The Lord gave us John 1:6 for him: "There came a man who was sent from God; his name was John." (NIV). We shared this verse with our son often when he was a child, and it was obvious that the good hand of God was upon him. Even at a very young age, he gravitated to the spiritual.

With every passing week, the Bible was coming more and more alive to me. Excited by my new discoveries about God and His Word, I tried to share them with Peggy. Although she was interested in spiritual matters, we began to realize that our faith was based on totally different foundations. I had a personal relationship with Jesus Christ based on my decision years earlier to make Him Savior and Lord of my life. Peggy knew about Jesus, but she didn't know Him personally and had not trusted Him for her salvation, relying instead on her good works. In subtle ways, we were drifting from each other, and I was burdened that Peggy should come to know the Lord personally.

One of my favorite radio programs was "The Gospel Hour," with Oliver B. Green, which I'd listen to each morning while driving to visit Mobil stations. Dr. Green was a powerful evangelist with a distinctive voice who had a way of penetrating deep into my spirit. He always shared his message with an energy and conviction that were contagious.

When "The Gospel Hour" began broadcasting a series of messages on Bible prophecy, I was fascinated and urged Peggy to listen. She did, and as a result, the Holy Spirit brought great conviction on her heart that if Jesus were to return, she would be left behind. The thought was so real to her that she would wake up in the middle of the night and reach over to see if I was still there, thinking the rapture had occurred and she missed it.

Then a crisis hit: Peggy contracted chicken pox while in the first trimester of pregnancy with our third child. It was the worst case the doctor had ever seen, and he said there was a fifty-fifty chance that our baby would be "seriously deformed."

Peggy was desperate and had no place to look but up. Miserable in body and spirit, she began to seriously examine her relationship with God, and faced the fact that her years of faithful service in the church would not save her. She was religious but eternally lost. In brokenness, she cried out to the Lord and received His free gift of eternal life based solely on His death on the cross, not on any good works she could perform.

Now we were united not only in marriage, but also in Christ—each for the other and both for the Lord. He would be the architect of our future...and of our family.

When Peggy gave birth to a perfectly healthy little girl on

September 9, 1960, we were thrilled. Arlene was perfectly formed, with no effects from Peggy's chicken pox. She was a miracle baby and an answer to our prayers, and we knew from the start that God had protected her for a very special reason.

Our involvement at Immanuel Baptist Church increased steadily in the years that followed. Pastor Richard Sueme was a true shepherd who fed us from God's Word each Sunday and challenged our hearts for world missions. As our interest continued to grow in the Great Commission—God's command in Matthew 28:19 to take the Gospel to the entire world—so did our longing to become more involved personally. The Lord reminded me of Don Gregory, one of my Marine instructors from Camp Lejeune. The reality of Don's faith, evidenced by his disciplined walk with God and his bold witness, had made a lasting impression on me.

I had no idea where Don lived, so I wrote to a Christian organization that he once was affiliated with, the Navigators, to see if they knew where he was. They sent me an address in Jacksonville, North Carolina, and I wasted no time in calling him. Don's desire to serve the Lord was as strong as ever. He had graduated from Columbia Bible College[2], married, and started a family. Don and his wife, Joan, were now missionaries with The Evangelical Alliance Mission (TEAM) planning to go to an unreached tribe in Dutch New Guinea, north of Australia.

We invited the Gregorys to visit us in Richmond, and they brought with them colorful slides of New Guinea. Peggy and I were fascinated as slide after slide seared our hearts. Don told us about the tribe they hoped to reach with the Gospel. The Asmat, or "true people" as the name translates, numbered about 50,000, and were scattered across the swampy marshes and mangrove thickets of the south coast of New

Guinea. Living a stone-age existence, the Asmat were canni-
bals who slept each night with their heads resting on the skulls
of their dead relatives. Newspapers were filled with reports of
Michael Rockefeller, son of Nelson Rockefeller, who had recently disappeared while collecting primitive art from the
Asmat tribe.

This was a people and a culture that was saturated with a
darkness that we knew nothing about. The outside world had
no clue the tribe even existed, let alone cared for their plight.
Yet, Don spoke with compassion for the desperate physical
and spiritual condition of a people who had never once heard
the Gospel. The images of these people of the jungle seemed
to cry out to me.

Don then paused and asked a question that burned in my
heart: "What is the cost for people like this to be reached?"

The projector clicked, advancing to the next slide. There,
on our living room wall, was a picture of two bodies being
carried out of the jungle.

Don told us how missionaries Walter Erikson and Edward
Tritt had gone on a survey patrol into the interior of New
Guinea's northern region. For seventeen days, they pushed
further and further into the jungle, hoping to make friendly
contact with some new tribes.

Accompanying them were five local men who grew increasingly fearful of a hostile encounter with the Asmats. The
men begged the missionaries to turn back. Frustrated and in
desperation, they took matters into their own hands. Early one
morning, while Erikson and Tritt were still asleep, the local
men cut the ropes of the missionaries' hammocks and beat
them to death with machetes and wooden clubs.

"Martyrdom was the price these missionaries paid so that
a tribe could hear the Gospel for the first time," Don told us.

I was stunned. The tragic deaths of Erikson and Tritt took

place in September 1952, just as I was finishing my training to go to Korea. All three of us were young, single Americans who had willingly taken risks for a cause greater than ourselves. I went to Korea to answer the call of my country; Erikson and Tritt went to New Guinea to answer the call of their Lord.

For the first time, I realized that missions is war, and sharing the Gospel is something worth dying for.

Peggy and I began contributing to the Gregorys' financial support so that they could take the Good News of Jesus Christ to the Asmat tribe. We had been looking for a missionary to "adopt" and support and were thrilled to finally do so. We also knew, however, that the Lord was calling us to something more. In the weeks that followed, we talked about little else than the possibility of going to the mission field ourselves. The appeal of Mobil's black gold was replaced by an urgency to reach our needy world for Christ.

My "territory," I realized, was not just Virginia. It was the world—a world where life-and-death odds didn't matter. The thought of engaging in a mission to rescue the spiritually lost from a fierce, unseen enemy was as compelling to me as our clandestine troop movements had been in Korea just a few years before. In the Marine Corps, I had been trained to give my life, if need be, for my country. Now I was ready to give my life for my Lord and His Kingdom.

Peggy shared my sense of urgency. We knew there was no higher calling, and we dreamed of being pioneers for the Lord among some needy people of the world—people like the Asmats who had never heard the Gospel.

I sent exploratory letters to several mission boards, sharing our desire to serve on the foreign mission field. It wasn't long before the responses arrived. They all seemed to say the same thing: Yes, we want you; but no, you don't meet our qualifications. One large mission to Africa sent a letter asking us:

[Do you have] any specialized Bible training such as you might get in a Bible institute or a Bible college, or did you attend Christian colleges where you might have had certain Bible courses?...We expect each of our applicants to be trained in the Bible.

The general director of another mission wrote:

When someone writes to say he is exploring the area of service for the Lord in the regions beyond, I...look for the items presented that may be considered as hurdles. We scan carefully one's qualifications, and one's lack of qualifications... Your case, as we have discussed it at Headquarters and have prayed about it, seems to be one that does have some *hurdles*... We accept no one unless he has had adequate preparation in systematic Bible study. I fail to find this in your case.

Hurdles! Having run track in high school, I understood the metaphor well. A hurdle is a barrier in the middle of a racetrack that a runner has to leap over during a race. Each letter seemed to mention another hurdle—I wasn't "qualified;" I was "too old;" Peggy and I had "too many children." Added together, they seemed insurmountable.

The only positive responses were invitations to apply for administrative jobs at mission headquarters in the U.S. That's not what Peggy and I wanted to do. We longed to go overseas, to be personally involved in reaching the unreached.

From my experience in the Marine Corps and with Mobil, I fully understood the need for a mission organization to maintain high standards and to make sure their members were prepared for the field. Yet, I wonder how things might have been different if only someone would have encouraged us in a personal way—or recognized the fact that while I didn't have formal Bible training, what I did know about the Scriptures had changed my life.

I wondered if my life was to become nothing more than the sum total of my sales figures—but I refused to be discouraged. Someone once said, "Nothing is really over until the moment you stop trying." That seemed to apply not just to my sales work, but also to our dream of becoming missionaries. I didn't want to give up.

Since all the mission boards said we needed Bible college training, that's where we would start. If I wanted to be missionary, it made sense to be grounded in the Word so that I really knew the Bible well. Peggy and I applied to Columbia Bible College in South Carolina.

Then we got the news that Peggy was pregnant with our fourth child—very exciting, but also very confusing to us. What was God saying? Wouldn't another child make it even harder for us to get to the field? Now that our other children were a little older, Peggy and I had both hoped to take classes, while I found a part-time job. With the prospect of four little ones to care for, however, the door to Bible college and the mission field seemed to be closing again.

Six weeks later, Peggy miscarried, and we suffered the loss of our precious baby. We were saddened, and any peace we had felt about going to Bible college evaporated. Maybe God was holding us back from the mission field because I wasn't "spiritual" enough. Did He want me to work in the business arena for the rest of my life? We didn't have a clue what God was saying. All we knew was that the burden to reach the world with the Gospel wasn't fading.

If we couldn't go to the field ourselves, we would get involved with as many missionaries as we could—supporting them, praying for them, and hosting them in our home. It wasn't hard to find quality missionaries to support; Immanuel Baptist had a mission family full of them. Among them was a couple our age that especially impressed us—Tom and Betsy Smoak. Tom was the guest speaker at church one Sunday, and when he walked up to the pulpit and turned toward us, we could see that his face was horribly scarred.

"What are you looking at?" Tom asked someone in the front row. He sounded completely serious, then told the audience, "Some of you don't look so good yourself."

A big grin broke out across his scarred face, putting us all at ease as a wave of laughter swept through the sanctuary.

Tom preached that morning about hell. He said that he knew what hell was like because he had recently experienced scorching flames. When he was in the Air Force, he took what was supposed to be a routine flight over Little Rock, Arkansas, but something went wrong. In a split second, fifty tons of liquid jet fuel ripped apart his B47 jet bomber. The other men in the fight crew were instantly killed, and Tom was blown out of the cockpit—his body on fire. Unconscious and falling, he had no chance of survival, when suddenly his parachute mysteriously deployed. It was full of holes, however, and Tom continued plummeting to earth.

A woman on the ground heard the explosion and spotted the fireball, flaming wreckage, and falling parachute. She pled for God to save whomever it was—and suddenly Tom started descending right into her yard. His tattered parachute draped itself over two large trees, as Tom's body slipped between them for a perfect landing on a concrete driveway.

Tom endured numerous surgeries to reconstruct his face and hands, which suffered third-degree burns. His sunglasses had protected his eyes, making it possible for him to continue his career in aviation. Eventually, he was discharged from the Air Force, but was able to become a missionary pilot and fly in

"God's Air Force." He and Betsy joined Wycliffe Bible Translators, a mission dedicated to translating God's Word into the languages of indigenous peoples around the world. They were raising support to go to Colombia, South America, where Tom would fly missionaries and supplies in and out of the jungle.

By now, God had blessed Peggy and me with four children: Ginny, John, Arlene, and our youngest daughter, Carol, who was born on March 29, 1963. After seven years with Mobil, a restlessness began to stir within me to pursue other opportunities. In December 1963, I was hired by Dow Jones and Company, the parent company of *The Wall Street Journal*, and accepted into their management training program in New York City. Once my training was complete, I was appointed as district manager of *The Wall Street Journal* in Washington, D.C. The Saturday before I started work, my brother Harry and I left a Gospel tract on every desk in the newsroom. On Monday morning, my first day at work, there was a memo on my desk with a copy of the tract that I had left. "Mr. Fletcher," the memo read, "the news department does not appreciate this literature."

The Lord blessed my efforts at the *Journal*, and after a few years, I was offered the position of district manager at the company's office in downtown New York. Peggy was getting pretty good at packing by this time, so once again we put everything into boxes and moved north.

My office was near Wall Street, close to the New York Stock Exchange. I loved working for Dow Jones, one of the most prestigious corporations in America. Each morning I traveled to work by ferry from New Jersey across New York's harbor, passing the majestic Statue of Liberty. What a reminder of my country's role as a place of refuge and hope for those who together built a mighty nation.

In the midst of a world of stocks and bonds, my vision for world evangelism never faded, but as the years went by, I was beginning to think that the dream was going to be fulfilled through our children. By now, they were all dedicated to the Lord Jesus and standing strong as a testimony among their friends. Their interest in missions didn't happen by accident. It was something Peggy and I deliberately nurtured in them. In fact, we prayed that God would call each of them to the mission field because we felt that missions was the highest calling that anyone could have in life. Table talks, casual conversations, and prayer times for far-off lands were a natural part of the children's lives. Our refrigerator door was covered with prayer cards and pictures of missionaries we knew around the world. We read books about missionaries, and as often as we could, we opened our home and hearts to missionaries—those who were home on furlough and those heading overseas for the first time. We always took special care to roll out the red carpet because we wanted to honor them.

Peggy and I knew that if our children were part of the process of hosting missionaries and spending their own money for missions, it would give them spiritual ownership over the projects they funded—involving not only their wallets, but their hearts as well. We set aside a big jar where our children "deposited" some of their mission money. As a group, they would decide whom to bless with the funds. For example, when one of our missionaries to Africa, Fran White, had to flee the Congo in 1964 because of unrest, she left all her possessions behind—including her Bible. Our children decided to spend some of their "jar" money to purchase a new Bible for Fran. When we saw her twenty years later, she still had that Bible.

Our children also sponsored needy children through World Vision. We started with Wawu Kalendi, a seven-year-old boy from Indonesia. His father was dead, and his destitute mother placed him in an orphanage so that his basic needs would be met. Ten months later, we "adopted" another Indonesian child, a little girl named Debra Wantania who was living in a children's home in West Java. Wawu's and Debra's photos also found their place on our refrigerator. These Indonesian children captured the hearts of our own children—and kept them beating for the nations.

Another missionary who became very dear to us when our family was young was Mary Baker, who served with Unevangelized Fields Mission in the Congo in Africa. Mary often stayed in our home while she was in the States on furlough. Short, warm, and outgoing, she worked alongside the national church helping to plant a church in a remote village called Benalia. Our church family supported her, prayed for her, and felt like we were on the field with her.

When violence broke out in 1964 following the Congo's independence, we were, of course, concerned for Mary's safety. There was no internet, e-mail, or fax service in those days, and news was slow in coming. We learned that gangs of young men, who called themselves Simba (meaning "lion" in Swahili) were terrorizing government and mission stations. Disillusioned and angry that independence had not made them wealthy, they sought to obliterate all vestiges of the West and carried out a drug-crazed campaign of terror—robbing, pillaging, torturing, and killing Congolese and foreigners alike.

Many missionaries left their stations for safer ground, but not Mary. She chose to stay with the people whom God had sent her to serve. Eventually, escalating tensions climaxed with an order to seize all Americans, and we feared she was among those taken hostage. Day after day, we kept up with TV and newspaper reports about the hostage crisis, and we were hopeful when Belgian paratroopers descended on the airport in the city of Stanleyville. Together with South African mercenaries, they managed to liberate the city from the hands of the rebels and free a number of hostages.

It took another three weeks for rescuers to fight their way to Benalia, some eighty miles to the north. They arrived, only to find that eleven missionaries had been killed—including our beloved Mary. One report said that rebels cut off Mary's limbs and her tongue. All the missionaries were either shot or hacked to death by machetes, and their bodies tossed into the Aruwimi River to be eaten by the crocodiles.

The sad news left us numb for weeks. Missions is war, I reminded myself, and the price can be costly. Sometimes a person pays with his or her life, but Scripture commends those who "did not love their lives so much as to shrink from death" (Revelation 12:11 NIV).

For some people that might have been a deterrent, but Mary's martyrdom only strengthened my resolve that world missions was where God was calling me, and that the price to be paid was worth the cost. Maybe it was the Marine in me. Maybe it was knowing that living for Christ was worth dying for.

God often sends influential people across our paths at pivotal crossroads in our lives. Mary was one of them. Dr. Gilbert J. McArthur was another. Gil was executive director of the South Sea Evangelical Mission in Australia, and a brilliant visionary. When he visited our home in 1968, he told us about the Christian Leaders' Training College (CLTC) in the highlands of Papua New Guinea—400 acres of almost uninhabitable swampland that he and others had transformed into the premier Christian training facility in the South Pacific. Gil was CLTC's first principal and was instrumental in raising the funds to keep it going. He wouldn't say it about himself, of course, but he was like a David Livingstone of the South Pacific—a pioneer who blazed paths that others followed. Peggy and I decided to sponsor a student to attend Christian Leaders' Training College, a young man named Silas Erikali.

Gil encouraged me to refuse to let go of my dream to become a missionary myself. He was a lone and welcome voice in the midst of many who were urging me to forget my dream and instead stick to making money to fund missions. The Lord knew that Gil was the right one to break through to me, and he confronted me with one of his favorite Scriptures: "We spend our years as a tale that is told" (Psalm 90:9 KJV).

"Ted, how are you writing the story of your life?" Gil asked me. "What is the next chapter that God might have for you?"

His question startled me, and in the weeks that followed, God wouldn't let me forget it. One May morning in 1968, I was alone in our Detroit, Michigan, living room reading my Bible, and when I came to Psalm 2:8, I stopped: "Ask of me, and I will make the nations your inheritance, the ends of the earth your possession" (NIV).

The words had such terrific authority that I knew God was speaking directly to me. I wrote in my Bible next to verse eight, "God's promise to me."

The words, of course, were originally a promise to the Messianic King, Jesus, that the domain of His Kingdom would someday extend around the world and include all the nations (or literally the "peoples") of the earth. The missionary task—sharing the Gospel and making disciples—was how God the Father would give the nations to His Son.

I also took this verse as a promise to me, and I knew that through it, God had come calling in my life. He was giving me a promise—and asking me to trust only Him, because humanly speaking there was no mechanism for its fulfillment.

Yet, nothing happened. No closed doors suddenly flew open. No mission board called to offer Peggy and me a position. All I had was a promise, and that's what I clung to for eight more long years in the corporate world—until once again the Lord spoke to me from Psalm 2:8. I again wrote "God's promise to me" in my Bible. By now, our son, John, had a clear call on his life to missions, and I again wondered if the promise would be fulfilled through him and our other children, rather than through Peggy and me. Despite my own sense of spiritual inadequacy, however, I knew God had a call on my life, too. I didn't know how He was going to do it, but His voice was unmistakable.

I knew it was futile to try to make something happen before it was God's timing. All my past attempts to serve God in full-time ministry had turned to dust, while everything I touched in the business world seemed to succeed. The Lord blessed my efforts at *The Wall Street Journal,* and we had record sales, and a topflight management team and sales staff. The Lord promoted me from district to regional sales manager in California, and then, at the age of thirty-nine, I became national sales manager for *The Wall Street Journal,* in charge of the sales force for the entire country. The Lord had given me a significant job with nationwide responsibility to maintain and increase the circulation of the *Journal.*

We moved back across country—from San Francisco to a nice home near Princeton, New Jersey, adjacent to Washington Crossing State Park. We had a pool and a little pond, and were close to good schools and our new congregation, Westerly Road Church. I loved the *Journal,* and the company was very good to me. Yet there was one question I pondered night and day: *What difference does it make how many people read* The Wall Street Journal *as far as eternity is concerned?*

The sense of safety in a secure corporate position meant

nothing to me. I knew the time had come to step outside my comfort zone—the same way people whom I loved and admired had done, people like Don and Joan Gregory, Tom and Betsy Smoak, Mary Baker, and Gil and Pat McArthur. Each could have taken the known road, but they were spiritual pioneers, following God's direction and blazing their own paths for others to follow.

The natural thing for Peggy and me to do would be to stay with the known and secure—but we knew if we ever wanted to see the fulfillment of God's promise, Psalm 2:8, in our lives, we had to obey and take the first step. In December 1973, I turned in my letter of resignation and sent a memo to my sales staff: "I have attempted to conduct my responsibilities in light of my personal faith in Jesus Christ. For me, the teachings and principles of the Bible have proven relevant and meaningful in my company life, as well as my personal life. I trust that you have seen these Christian principles attend the discharge of my professional duties."

My years at *The Wall Street Journal* had been a mission field of sorts, but now God was calling me out of my "Jerusalem" to points unknown, to places unseen, to people unreached. As I left *The Journal* for the last time, it was with a deep sense of gratitude for all that the Lord had done.

I'd love to say that He immediately opened the door to missions, but there were no big checks or letters of invitation waiting in the mailbox when I returned home that evening. Instead, I began what people often call the "wilderness wanderings." I knew God was calling me to missions; He had made that very clear. Yet, for reasons known only to Him, He required me to go through a wilderness experience before I could fulfill that call.

This wandering went on for four years, in fact. While I waited for God to fulfill His plan, I worked as vice president

for Western Temporary Services; at a car dealership that I
owned with my brothers, Waller and Bill; as assistant to the
president of Washington Bible College, and as marketing director at Gospel Light Publishing Company in southern
California. I knew God placed me in those positions as part of
His plan for my life, but it was frustrating to wait while my
heart burned for missions and the call to world evangelization.

During those years, I often thought of Joseph, Moses,
Esther, Paul, and others in the Bible to whom God gave a distinct call, but required them to wait years before fulfilling it.
Joseph languished in an Egyptian jail. Moses wandered in the
desert. Esther waited while her people seemed destined for destruction. Paul was arrested, jailed, and beaten.

God knew what was ahead for them, of course, and He
knew what was ahead for me. He knew I would need an even
deeper faith in Him for the challenges that were around the
corner.

CHAPTER 5

Genesis of an Idea

By faith Abraham, when called to go to a place he would later receive as his inheritance, obeyed and went, even though he did not know where he was going.
—Hebrews 11:8 (NIV)

Do all the good you can, by all the means you can, in all the ways you can, in all the places you can, at all the times you can, to all the people you can, as long as ever you can.
—John Wesley

"We are desperate. We are dying!"
This was no slick, glossy fund-raising letter I was holding. It was composed on a manual typewriter, addressed to Peggy and me, and mailed from Nigeria—a personal letter from our friend Joshua Ekpikhe. We'd met Joshua a few years earlier at Washington Bible College (WBC). His ministry in Nigeria, called Christian Witness Team (CWT), had impressed me so deeply that I raised money from my extended family to con-

struct the first medical facility in Joshua's area of southern Nigeria.

We had kept up quite a correspondence with this national leader and were always excited to follow the growth and fruit of his ministry. With this latest letter, he wasn't asking for more money. That would have been easy. He was asking for *us*.

> Ted and Peggy,
>
> Please give at least two years of your lives to help us. The Christian Witness Team is too big for me to manage and develop right now...I need a man behind the scenes to lean upon in every area of the team administratively...
>
> Nigerian Christians and non-Christians alike are crying, "Give us something to read!" If the Church will not respond, the communists are! This is the time for American Christians to help. Next year might be too late.
>
> We are desperate. We are dying!

Joshua had sent us more than a letter; it was a Macedonian call. I felt like Paul must have in Acts chapter 16 when a man from Macedonia appeared to him in a vision and begged him, "Come over and help us." As Peggy and I prayed for wisdom during the months that followed, Joshua's plea began to create in us a compelling call to service. God had come calling—through His messenger, a humble Nigerian believer.

We had just recently applied to a well-known mission that had a reputation for working in unevangelized areas of the world. My brother John was on their board of directors, and we liked their vision for ministry. With my background in business, I thought there might be a place for me on the field. I applied and even included the results of a psychological profile I had taken at a Christian company. The profile described me as a goal-oriented person who was willing to take risks. To me, that sounded like exactly what a mission board should want—someone who thought outside the box.

To our amazement, the mission rejected us. I certainly didn't think I was the Lord's gift to the mission field, but I couldn't believe with my experience that there wasn't a spot to plug me in. Obviously, the more traditional mission agencies, which were used to doing things the same way they always had, weren't ready for someone to come in and disturb the status quo.

As I considered our options, I talked with Dr. William Miller, a friend who was dean of students at WBC. He was a mobilizer at heart, and consistently encouraged me not to give up my dream. This time, however, his words went beyond encouragement; he asked a question that surprised me: "Why don't you start your own mission board?"

Could someone who was rejected by several mission boards start his *own*? The more Peggy and I talked it over, the more we felt that's exactly what the Lord was calling us to do. The clincher came one day in prayer when the Lord reminded me of the promise He had given from Psalm 2:8—"Ask of me, and I will make the nations your inheritance, the ends of the earth your possession" (NIV).

This time, however, He added something more: "Ted, I've given you the promise. Now take it by faith."

From a practical standpoint, the timing made sense. Our lives were much less complicated now that our three oldest children were at WBC preparing for the mission field. Ginny had already gone to Mexico as a summer missionary and also felt a stirring to full-time missions. John had gone to Irian Jaya, Indonesia (formerly Dutch New Guinea), on a summer mission trip, and knew God was calling him to full-time service. Arlene was at WBC, planning on mission work. Only Carol, our fifteen-year-old daughter, was at home with us, and she was already looking forward to Bible college.

God's leading was clear. He was calling our entire family into missions. Now was the time. We decided that the Washington, D.C., area was the best place to base our operations. We already had a great relationship with WBC, and we'd be near all the foreign embassies. Most importantly, our spiritual home was there, Faith Bible Church in Sterling, Virginia, where my brother John served as senior pastor. We needed the guidance and support of this unique church family, and a church with such a strong emphasis on world missions would be the perfect fit.

I made plans to go to Nigeria to survey the work and see how we could become involved in training and mobilizing nationals. In November 1978, Peggy and I mailed our first prayer letter to share our plan to work with Joshua Ekpikhe and CWT:

> Peggy and I are enthusiastic about the great opportunity God has given us to help train national workers to reach some of the more than 80 million Nigerians with the Gospel of our Lord. The Nigerian cry today is the same cry that existed in Jeremiah's day: "The harvest is past, the summer has ended, and we are not saved" (Jeremiah 8:20 NIV). We are trusting the Lord for our monthly support and travel needs. I am convinced that the Lord who has brought us thus far will see us to the end. He cannot fail.

Four days into 1979, I boarded a Pan Am jet and took off for Nigeria. What a way to start the new year! In my two decades in the business world, I had been on plenty of planes—but this time was different. There was such a sense of God's leading, that He had "divine appointments" already lined up, and in spite of the years of waiting, His plans were not a moment late.

My traveling companions were George Miles, president of WBC; Don Darling, chairman of the board of Faith Bible Church; and Ralph Sauers, Sr., whose son was serving with the CWT as a missionary teacher. We landed in the capital city, Lagos, and made our way to the village of Ikwa, home of CWT. Joshua was glad to see us, and we were excited to be there.

Our first day began with dedicating the Fletcher Memorial Clinic and the Virginia E. Fletcher Nurses' Residence, named after my parents. The clinic was the first medical facility for the 25,000 people living in the area, and was destined to become an effective evangelistic center. Already, parents were lined up with their sick children—kids who could easily die without medical attention.

For the next six and a half weeks, I saw other tremendous needs. At the Bible and Missionary Theological College, one of the CWT ministries, I talked with as many students as I could. Most were young Nigerians seeking to become better equipped for ministry. Never before had I seen such dedication for reaching a lost world. In fact, three of them told me about their desire to go to Indonesia as missionaries, but there was no church, mission board, or money to send them. Was there a way, I wondered, that we could help them?

The CWT ministry was certainly creative—a bakery, welding shop, sawmill, several bookstores, and the largest printing press for Christian literature in Nigeria. Each of these provided outreach opportunities, jobs for believers, and funds to operate the ministry. Evangelism, of course, was at the heart of everything they did. I joined students from the Bible college as they visited villages; they expected God to save people, and He did! It was absolutely amazing. In one mud hut, five family members knelt down on their dirt floor and gave their lives to Christ.

We visited other strategic areas throughout Nigeria, conducting open-air evangelistic meetings. About forty percent of Nigeria is Muslim, and this was the first time I had ever really met Muslims. They were amazingly similar to anyone else without the Lord, and as I preached and Joshua gave the invitation, the Holy Spirit moved on the hearts of the people. In one place, 1,000 people showed up in an open field—without any advance publicity. More than 200 of them responded to the invitation for salvation, and many waited until late at night just to be prayed with individually. In another village, the local chief was among those who rose to his feet for salvation.

We also ministered in a prison where forty men, many bound with chains on their hands and feet, were crammed into a stifling hot cell. Some were awaiting trial, and if convicted would be immediately executed by a firing squad. I spoke to them from John 8:36—"If the Son sets you free, you will be free indeed" (NIV). Regardless of their chains, I told them, Jesus Christ could set them free from their sins and deliver them. When I gave the invitation, I'll never forget the clanging of chains as the men threw themselves forward with their faces on the ground and cried out to Christ for salvation. When we were ready to leave, these prisoners who needed everything—food, medicine, and clothing—asked me for just one thing: Bibles.

Of all the thousands of people we saw in Nigeria, there's one person I'll never forget: a pathetic man who was begging by the side of the road. He looked as if he could easily have been demon-possessed, and I felt unusual compassion toward him. He was a human being with a soul, a man for whom Christ died. His plight spoke powerfully of a lost world of people who have been crippled and blinded by sin and held captive by Satan. I told him about the One who loved him and gave His life for him.

As we waited at the airport for our flight back to the U.S., God set up one final divine appointment, and I had the opportunity to lead a Muslim security agent to Christ.

It was a trip that opened my eyes, tugged at my heart, and expanded my faith. God was directing me in ways I couldn't see. For six weeks, I had seen God work in ways that I never dreamed possible. It was the power of the Gospel. For the first time in my life, I felt as if I was involved in the most important work in the world.

I came home with a burden for the lost and a sense of urgency that all people everywhere might hear one simple message—the Good News of Jesus Christ. This was Peggy's vision, too, and she was as excited as I was about what the Lord was saying to us. Ever since that day back in 1960 when Peggy fully gave her life to the Lord, we were one in purpose and vision. We now knew that God was giving us a blueprint for action to establish a mission agency. We would begin with the ministry in Nigeria as a pilot project, and expand to other strategic areas as God led, focusing on mobilizing and training nationals. In Nigeria, God had shown me first-hand how vital and effective this strategy could be. Joshua was doing an amazing job in his own country. Where we could, it made sense to send missionaries to help support the work that national pastors, leaders, evangelists, and church planters were already doing.

In the basement of our home—our first office—we sat

down at the drawing board to sketch out a plan. We came up with a name for the new mission: World Evangelical Outreach. "World" described the extent of our vision; "evangelical" emphasized our solid commitment to the Gospel and biblical truth, and "outreach" revealed our heart to penetrate areas beyond the existing borders of Christian witness. Our vision was Romans 15:20, to "preach the gospel where Christ was not known" (NIV).

Not everyone shared the vision. One mission leader rather bluntly asked, "Who would have the audacity to start another mission board?" Another said, "We already have enough mission agencies." A seminary professor suggested we had chosen the wrong name. "Why don't you call yourselves *Africa* Evangelical Outreach?" he asked me.

"Because God has given us the world," I responded. God's promise to me was clear: "I will make the nations your inheritance" (Psalm 2:8 NIV).

It must have seemed ludicrous to some that a person with no formal theological training was now the self-appointed general director of a mission with a global-sounding name, but absolutely no missionaries. Yet we were seeing our new mission with eyes of faith, and, thankfully, the Lord kept bringing us others who had similar vision. In the weeks that followed, we shared our plans with every pastor and church who would listen, starting at our own church, Faith Bible. Invitations came and doors opened for us.

We wrote our statement of faith, organized a board of directors and an advisory committee, and photocopied brochures describing our founding vision and principles. At our first board meeting, we decided that prayer was to be our priority, and included this declaration in our by-laws:

All that follows in these by-laws comes only after prayer. Prayer is always to be the first priority, the

*PIONEERS first "office" in the
basement of our home*

*First overseas trip together, in
the highlands of Papua New
Guinea, 1979*

*With J. Oswald
Sanders, Gil
MacArthur,
Leonard Buck,
and David Price
at Christian
Leaders' Training
College, Papua
New Guinea,
1979.*

*With Biami tribe in Papua New Guinea. "And there, where they were living,
I sat among them for seven days overwhelmed"* (Ezekiel 3:15 NIV).

highest purpose, the moving force, the vital energizer of this Mission. The overriding prerequisite in every provision of these by-laws is earnest, travailing prayer to the Father that the world might hear of His Son through our hearts and lips, made ready by prayer.

All who serve the Lord with this organization are charged with this sacred trust—to pray for the blessed will of the Father to be accomplished through us.

At that first board meeting, we elected Don Darling chairman and decided that our focus would be to mobilize national workers to go to the most needy people of the world. We would represent both CWT in Nigeria and also the Christian Leaders' Training College (CLTC) in Papua New Guinea, a move that was strongly suggested by Gil McArthur, one of CLTC's founders and my good friend who had challenged me for missions more than a decade earlier. We launched a student scholarship program linking American Christians with national students on the field, and we also started raising funds for strategic projects.

We also decided to mobilize American missionaries in partnership with their local sending churches. In fact, at that first board meeting we accepted our very first career missionaries: Ruth Wright, a nurse, to oversee the medical clinic in Nigeria, and Carol Baur, a gifted Bible teacher, to teach at the CWT Bible college in Nigeria. And finally, we appointed our first summer missionaries, our daughter, Ginny, and son, John, who would spend part of the summer working at CLTC in Papua New Guinea.

Within two months of that first board meeting, eight missionary candidates approached us about serving in various remote locations around the world, and we wondered what countries God might have for us next. Gil was anxious to get us more involved in the South Pacific, so Peggy and I decided to travel there in late summer, heading first to Australia, then to Papua New Guinea to join Gil and attend CLTC council meetings.

Travel agents say that Papua New Guinea is "like every place you've never been." About 100 miles north of Australia, the country is the eastern half of the second largest island in the world. It has a population of more than 4 million people divided into about 800 tribes, each with its own language and customs.

While Papua New Guinea had a lot of attention from foreign missionaries, there were still small primitive tribes buried deep in the jungle and cut off from the outside world. Peggy and I were anxious to visit some of these tribal areas. Although every flight to the Southern Highlands was booked, God miraculously opened the door for us to find a Mission Aviation Fellowship plane to fly us into the interior. The flight to Mougulu seemed to take us back in time a couple of thousand years, which is probably why Papua New Guinea is called "the land that time forgot." The people we found in that remote place were just emerging from a stone-age existence. Some of them still practiced cannibalism, and in fact, just a few weeks before our arrival at one village, members of a neighboring village had killed and eaten two women. It seemed impossible that people who appeared so gentle to us were capable of raiding a village at night, and killing and eating other humans.

We spent a few days at Mougulu with Tom and Salome Hoey, Australian missionaries with Asia Pacific Christian Mission (APCM). They poured out their hearts to us about nine other tribes in the Western Province that were still unreached. The tribes ranged from a few hundred people to a few thousand. Each had its own distinct language, unknown to the outside world. The area was desolate with mosquito-infested swamps, poisonous snakes, and sweltering heat. Over the years, APCM had difficulty attracting missionaries to work in these smaller tribes. Our hearts were burdened for these lost people, and Peggy and I began praying right away that God would allow us to recruit workers for them.

From Papua New Guinea, we traveled to the neighboring Solomon Islands, site of major battles during World War II where many gave their lives on the sands of Guadalcanal. Peggy and I came to the Solomons to view the ministries of the South Sea Evangelical Mission and the national church. Among the many people we met were two distinguished citizens: Sir Peter Kenilorea, the country's prime minister, who graciously invited us to his home for dinner, and Silas Erikali, the young man we had financially supported back in 1968 when he was a student at CLTC. Now he was principal of a Bible college!

It was another extraordinary trip full of God's leading and divine appointments. We were amazed at the number of people whom God had linked us up with years earlier who were now so strategic as we set up our new mission—Gil MacArthur, Leonard Buck, Bill Clack, and Oswald Sanders in the South Pacific, and Joshua Ekpikhe in Nigeria. We were beginning to see how God had been working in our lives during all the years when we thought nothing was happening.

Not long after we returned home, I met with Dr. Ralph Winter, a world-renowned missiologist who, with his wife, Roberta, had recently founded the U.S. Center for World Mission in Pasadena, California. A few years earlier, Dr. Winter had dropped a spiritual bombshell on the mission community, which had gathered at the historic Congress on World Evangelization in Lausanne, Switzerland. More than 2,700 mission and church leaders from all over the world had assembled to talk, strategize, and pray about missions. In a plenary address, Dr. Winter presented a paper entitled *The Highest Priority: Cross-Cultural Evangelism,* in which he argued quite convincingly that a staggering 2.4 billion people were living beyond the range of the Gospel. If our present missionary strategy didn't change, Dr. Winter warned the leaders, these people would never have a chance to hear the Gospel in their own language or within their own culture.

He then identified five major blocks of "hidden peoples" as he called them: Chinese, Muslim, Hindu, Buddhist, and Tribal.[3] He insisted that the only way to reach these "hidden peoples" was with a fresh cross-cultural approach to evangelism. He cautioned that this endeavor had to become the highest priority of the Church if we were to finish the task that Jesus gave to us.

In Nigeria, we had learned the importance of working with national leaders. In the South Pacific, the Lord showed us first-hand the importance of reaching the unreached. My life had always gravitated to the front lines—in war, business, and now in missions. I felt as if our new mission, which was only in its infancy, was part of a new idea, and that the idea was from God: to focus on people in unreached areas, those with the least opportunity to hear the Gospel, regardless of how dangerous or how difficult the task might be. I had no interest whatsoever in duplicating what other mission boards were doing or "treading on their territory." I wanted us to be on the cutting edge of what God was doing, with a focus as crystal clear as that of Paul, the missionary: "It has always been my ambition to preach the gospel where Christ was not known, so that I would not be building on someone else's foundation" (Romans 15:20 NIV). If God would raise up a team, we would go.

We had already chosen Psalm 96:3 for our letterhead:

"Declare his glory among the nations" (NIV). We liked this verse because it communicated God's desire to bless the peoples of the earth with His glory. Nations aren't the same as countries. A country is a geographical unit, such as France, Papua New Guinea, or Brazil. The word *nation,* or *ethne,* however, is used in Scripture to refer to people—people groups such as the fifty different ethnic groups living in Senegal, or the 490 people groups in China. Each has its own language and culture. God sent His Son to reach not countries but "nations" of ethno-linguistic people groups. In fact, the Great Commission tells us to "go and make disciples of all *nations"* (Matthew 28:19 NIV, emphasis added).

We were beginning to realize that the task of world evangelization was a lot more complex than just saying, "Let's send another missionary to Indonesia." The need was not just more missionaries, but more missionaries going to the right places.[4] So with this emphasis on unreached peoples, we immediately began to recruit new missionaries to go to people groups in the five blocks that Dr. Winter mentioned. Our start in Nigeria enabled us to touch the Muslim block, and God was strategically linking us with unreached tribes in Papua New Guinea. But what of the other blocks—Hindu, Buddhist, and Chinese? How would God open a door for us to reach them?

CHAPTER 6

Small Beginnings

Do not despise these small beginnings, for the Lord rejoices to see the work begin.
    —Zechariah 4:10 (NLT)

I am only one, but I am one. I cannot do everything, but I can do something. And what I can do, I ought to do. And what I ought to do, by God's grace I will do.
    —Anonymous

I've always liked history, and one of my favorite bits of trivia is this brief entry from the diary of England's King George III: "Nothing much happened today."

The date was July 4, 1776. King George might have thought nothing much happened that day, but we know better. A few American patriots bravely signed a document asserting their freedom—a document that could easily have been their death warrant. What looked like a small, insignificant piece of paper to the king set off a revolution that changed history.

I also like biblical history, and one of my favorite Scripture verses is from Zechariah chapter 4 when Zerubbabel was rebuilding the temple: "Then he [the angel] said to me, 'This is what the Lord says to Zerubbabel: It is not by force nor by strength, but by my Spirit, says the Lord Almighty...Do not despise these small beginnings, for the Lord rejoices to see the work begin, to see the plumb line in Zerubbabel's hand'" (Zechariah 4: 6, 9-10 NLT).

To some people, our new mission might have looked like a "small beginning," but the Lord continually reminded me not to despise the day of small beginnings. Like Zerubbabel rebuilding the temple, we were laying the foundation, but we knew the job wasn't going to get done by our might or power—only by the Spirit of the Lord.

There was no manual we could read on how to start a mission. The only experience I could rely on was the teamwork I learned in the Marine Corps, and the know-how I gained at Mobil Oil Company and *The Wall Street Journal* about relying on the Lord to ensure that a venture would prosper and grow.

Just as those enterprises started small, so did this new mission, but the Lord was about to expand our work beyond anything we could have dreamed. It began in a very "small" way—a casual conversation with Harry Liu, a Chinese-American missionary whom I had met a number of years earlier. Harry was in town for a mission conference at Faith Bible Church. It was just a few weeks after my meeting with Dr. Ralph Winter, and I couldn't get out of my mind the one billion unreached people living in the People's Republic of China. At that time, China was just beginning to open after the devastating Cultural Revolution and was still suspicious of foreigners and intolerant of Christians. Chinese believers who managed to survive the Cultural Revolution were severely persecuted, and faced arrest, torture, imprisonment, and even death.

With Peggy on the Great Wall, 1987

Below: Witnessing to communist guards in China, 1987

Peggy in Cambodia, 1999

With Harry Liu, 1981

PIONEERS *International Leadership Conference, Thailand, 1999*

Needless to say, missionaries were forbidden to enter the country. You just couldn't walk up to the Chinese Embassy and ask for a visa to evangelize in Tiananmen Square. Of course, most unreached peoples live in countries that don't grant missionary visas. But Jesus didn't say, "Go into the parts of the world where you can get a missionary visa." He just said, "Go into *all* the world."

When I asked Harry Liu how we could get Christian English teachers into China, his response was simple: "We make friends." Harry explained that nothing happens in China apart from relationships. We had to make some friends, and Harry knew just how to do it.

The next thing I knew we were in my car driving to the Chinese Embassy in downtown Washington, D.C. Here I was, head of a Christian mission agency that wanted access to the people of a highly suspicious, communist, and atheist country so that I could share the Gospel with them, and Harry was taking me right to their embassy. Of course, Harry didn't tell them that. He introduced me as a former businessman who was interested in helping relations between the U.S. and China. And he introduced himself as a teacher. (After the meeting was over, I said, "Harry, I didn't know you were a teacher in China," and he replied with a smile, "I was—a Bible teacher! ")

Harry asked the receptionist if we could meet with the person who was in charge of placing English teachers in China. We were ushered into a room beautifully decorated with Chinese carvings, where we met with a man I'll call Mr. Cheng—who was in charge of recruiting English teachers for China!

Mr. Cheng had just recently arrived in the U.S. and seemed incredibly nervous even talking with us. After all, not too many Americans walked in off the streets just to make friends. Harry started talking with him in Mandarin, trying to make him feel at ease as he explained our love of China and desire to help.

Harry also had a guaranteed door-opener in his pocket: a letter on White House stationery signed by President Carter's national security advisor, Zbigniew Brzezinski. The letter had nothing to do with me, but Brzezinski mentioned Harry...and I was Harry's friend. Harry was a master at seizing an opportunity, and he planned to use that letter to the fullest. It seemed to give both of us official status, as if we were important people with connections in high places.

As Harry and Mr. Cheng chatted, they discovered they were from the same city in China—a city, it turned out, that needed westerners to come and teach English. By the end of our meeting, Mr. Cheng asked me to help find them! God had performed a miracle.

It proved what Peggy and I believed—that there was no such thing as a "closed" country, and if the doors seem to be closed, we should check the windows. Maybe some people thought we were naïve (we certainly didn't have enough experience under our belts to make us experts), but we sincerely believed that God would open doors to enter these so-called "closed" countries, and give us the strategies for evangelism and church planting. After all, we weren't going to these difficult-to-reach peoples because they wanted us. We were going because God wanted them!

Once the red-lacquered doors to mainland China had swung wide open for us, we immediately began recruiting and sending English teachers to take advantage of this incredible opportunity. Meanwhile, our relationship with Mr. Cheng grew, and he became a friend of our family, giving each of our children pet names. In fact, whenever he called our home, he would insist on talking with each of them—not only to practice his English-language skills, but also to develop a relationship with his new American friends. He would often read us accounts that he had written about his daily experiences in the U.S. We had many opportunities to share our faith with him. He once asked Arlene, "Do you think God would forgive me for some terrible things I've done in my life?" She assured him that our Lord is full of mercy, always ready to forgive a repentant sinner who turns to Christ for salvation.

Years later when my son, John, and I were in Beijing, we had dinner with Mr. Cheng and his son at a hotel restaurant. He gave us a beautiful vase as a gift. It must have cost him a month's salary to honor us in such a gracious way. He knew we were Christians, and possibly was even aware of what we were really doing, but he also knew we loved China. He had obviously grown to love us, too, and appreciate our friendship, as we did his.

At the same time that God cracked open the window for us to the world's most populous country, He was also widening the door He had already opened for us in Papua New Guinea—this time to tribes that had very little, if any, contact with the Gospel.

How did we recruit missionaries willing to live in a snake-infested jungle, survive under primitive conditions, and befriend tribal people whose cultures were rooted in cannibalism? The answer is that God found them for us. Not long after we returned from our 1979 trip to Papua New Guinea and began aggressively recruiting missionaries to live among the unreached tribes there, God sent us Vance and Patty Woodyard. We had met the Woodyards before they were even married—while they were students at Washington Bible College where our three oldest children attended. Vance and Patty were members of the Islands of the Sea prayer band, which met regularly to intercede for the unreached tribal peoples of the world. They told us they wanted to become missionaries to an unreached tribe. I contacted Bob Callaghan, who was general director of Asia Pacific Christian Mission (APCM) in Australia, and recommended them. In January 1980, I was delighted to receive his quick response inviting Vance and Patty to spend a year with APCM working in the Biami tribe, which Peggy and I had visited the year before.

It was gratifying that Bob Callaghan and APCM welcomed our missionaries as full members, especially at a time when many other mission agencies had reservations about us, in part because our missionaries were all young and untested. When we had nothing more than a vision and a handful of missionaries, APCM helped us get our first team established. In fact, Bob said he hoped this was the beginning of "deeper fellowship" between our two missions—exactly what we wanted to hear. We felt our visions were compatible and were happy to work with them and to learn from them. We eventually set up a working agreement for our missionaries to be "seconded" (loaned) to the APCM team in Papua New Guinea.

That summer, our daughter Arlene went to Papua New Guinea on a summer team through APCM. She was just a teenager at the time, and Peggy and I will never forget one of her letters home describing a trek through the jungle where she saw a human skull hanging from a tree. That would have been challenging enough for a teenager, but then she learned that the person had been eaten by the very man who was guiding her team through the jungle. I'm sure many people could not understand how Peggy and I would let our young daughter travel in such a rough place, but we had long ago given back our children to the Lord, knowing He could do a much better job watching out for them than we could. It was actually a privilege to see Arlene step out into the unknown so early in life, knowing that God was guiding her steps.

Arlene loved Papua New Guinea, and so did Vance and Patty. The Woodyards had signed up to work there for a year, and during that time the Lord gave them a burden for the Konai, an unreached tribe of about 600 people who had had only limited contact with westerners. Outgoing and friendly, they could also be volatile and belligerent, but they won the Woodyards' hearts. Vance and Patty eventually returned to live among them, continuing that ministry for thirteen years.

A lot of prayer went into the Woodyards' work. Their older children grew up knowing the jungle as their only home, and the Konai as their playmates. The family learned the un-written language, and Vance and Patty analyzed the language and developed an alphabet so that they could begin translating the Scriptures. By the time the Woodyards left Papua New Guinea thirteen years later, more than 150 Konai had come to Christ, and many of the new Christians were even reaching out to their former enemies. There was a Bible school, disci-pleship program, and some translated portions of Scripture. A team from Wycliffe Bible Translators is now completing the Konai New Testament.

The wonderful story of reaching the Konai started with a "day of small beginnings"—something that we would see re-peated in resistant areas all over the world. The work in India, for example, began with numbers that seemed overwhelming: a country of nearly one billion people, with thirty babies born every minute, most of whom will live and die serving Hindu gods.

How could we ever reach such a vast country with 3,000 people groups (2,900 considered unreached), 600,000 vil-lages, 33 million Hindu gods, and 200 million sacred cows?

Through our work in Nigeria, we knew how effective it

was to work with national Christian leaders. In India, even though the numbers of unreached were formidable, there was already a small, but significant, number of national Christians and Christian ministries at work. If someone could provide them with resources and help mobilize them, they could reach India for Christ.

Nothing has ever given me more of a sense of the degradation of lost humanity than the streets of Calcutta. John and I walked them in 1980 with Dr. Philip Steyne, a mission professor at Columbia Bible College and Seminary and a new member of our board of directors. Beggars to my right and to my left quickly formed a chain behind us as we pressed forward through the hordes of people. Their broken lives and mutilated bodies bore little testament of the fact that they were created in God's image. Standing on Howrah Bridge and looking toward the city, we saw a mass of humanity. An average of five bodies a day wash up on the banks of the Hoogley River, usually to be eaten by wild dogs. Death was visible at every point—and no wonder. Calcutta is named after Kali, the Hindu goddess of death and destruction, and she is so highly revered in this city that she has a death grip on the 12 million people who live there and worship her.

We were also moved in ways that are hard to describe when we went to Mother Teresa's House of Dying Destitutes. This was a city—and a country—that needed the love and power of Jesus. There was no other hope.

We returned from India with heavy, yet hopeful, hearts, knowing we had to do something to help evangelize the unreached in this vast country. Once again, God gave us a strategy, and then began linking us with the people to get the job done—starting with Samuel Paulson, an Indian national. Our children had been fellow students with Sam at Washington Bible College. After graduation, he returned to India with a vision to mobilize 1,000 workers to plant churches in 1,000 villages. Needless to say, Sam was just the kind of national leader with whom we wanted to work.

At that time, India was still closed to outside ministries and missionaries, but Sam knew many national workers in India who were trained and excited about reaching their country for Christ. They had the zeal but lacked some of the basics. Many, for example, rode bicycles or walked from village to village because they couldn't afford cars, motorbikes, or even public transportation. India was a strategic challenge with so many unreached people, but if we could mobilize the national workers, they could get the job done much better than we could. We knew that the Lord was showing us another open door, and by our spring 1981 board meeting, Sam and his wife, Rachel, became our first non-Western members. Sam was especially encouraged by my brother-in-law Jack Hoey, who helped to expand Sam's contacts with local churches in the United States and undergird the ministry financially. In the next two decades, Sam, Rachel, and their national workers would plant 300 churches in India.

One more significant event occurred during that 1980 trip to India. John and I went to Nepal, where we took a bus ride across the Himalayas to the border with mainland China. We couldn't cross the border, but we wanted to get as close to China as possible. As we looked across the Friendship Bridge that linked the two countries, I could see some Chinese soldiers pacing back and forth, watching us as we watched them. Suddenly, I had a flashback to thirty years earlier when I was in Korea. I had seen Chinese soldiers there, too, but then they were the enemy and I was trying to kill them. Now I desperately wanted to meet these soldiers, befriend them, and share the love of Jesus with them. For the moment, however, that was impossible. All we could do was bow our heads and pray quietly that God would open the doors to this great country and that multitudes would come to know His love.

A year later, Peggy and I took our first trip to China together, joined by Harry and Bertha Liu and Phil Steyne. Like every trip we had taken, this one opened our eyes and enlarged our hearts. The guidebooks didn't mention it, and the handful of tourists didn't see it, but China was in the midst of a spiritual revolution. Christians who had survived the horrendous years of the Cultural Revolution were now taking on the task of evangelizing their country, and the church was growing at an astonishing rate, in spite of severe persecution. Whenever Christians have been persecuted throughout history, the church has grown, and China was no exception. When the communists took over in 1949, all foreign missionaries were expelled from the country, and there were only about 5 million Chinese Christians in the entire country. By 1976, the end of the Cultural Revolution, many of these Christians were killed or imprisoned, but the persecution purified and strengthened the indigenous church. Now, in the summer of 1981, nobody knew how many Christians there were—only that the number was growing rapidly.

God was doing something extraordinary in this "closed" land, and we wanted to be part of it. As we packed for that trip, we loaded our luggage with Bibles and other Christian materials, which we planned to secretly distribute to underground Chinese Christians. This was totally illegal, according to Chinese law (it still is). So our first challenge was to get our luggage through customs without anyone spotting our precious cargo, and the second was to deliver everything to the underground Christians without getting them or us arrested. We didn't have a clue how we would do either, but, thankfully, God had a plan.

When our plane landed in Shanghai, however, we had to

wonder what God was planning because the customs area was a sea of open suitcases, with clothing and personal belongings strewn everywhere. As the line of passengers inched forward, stern Chinese police were meticulously going through every piece of luggage—and our turn was rapidly approaching. In a few moments, they would find the Bibles and we would be in big trouble.

Suddenly I heard a voice calling in English, "Mr. Fletcher, over here, please." I turned to see a young Chinese woman who approached us and smiled. She shook hands with all of us, and bowed and nodded a couple of times, and then said our car was waiting. While we stood there mystified, she said something in Chinese to the customs clerk, who nodded in return. Before we knew it, our luggage was collected, and we were whisked to the front of the line and out the door. Our suitcases were never opened, and our Bibles were safely inside communist China.

As we drove off, we learned the reason for this red-carpet treatment. Before we left for China, Harry had telegrammed a Shanghai business contact of my brother Bill, saying that we were coming to visit his city, and letting him know our arrival date and flight number. The young woman explained that she worked at that company and was at our service during our stay in Shanghai.

God did indeed have a plan. The next day, we were the honored guests at a dinner hosted by a group of Shanghai business and government leaders. To my further astonishment, I was asked to pray over the dinner! I prayed and gave thanks for the food, and Harry gave each person a bilingual Gospel of John.

Later that week, we secretly met with underground Chinese pastors and gave them the Scriptures we had brought into the country. They were so grateful to receive the literature. One dear pastor had been horribly tortured for his faith, and his crippled hands were disfigured with knuckles that had been broken by police. His faith was passionate and all consuming, with no cost too great for the sake of the Savior.

A Chinese believer in another city arranged for us to visit a small "house church," one of the secret congregations where even today Chinese Christians risk their lives to meet and worship. We walked down narrow back streets, making sure we weren't followed, then up three flights of dark stairs and into a crowded room where an electrifying meeting was already underway. Just as we entered, a woman was reading a letter she had received that day, announcing that a Christian from America named "Brother Ted" would be coming for a visit with his wife and friends.

Imagine their surprise and ours when we walked in just at that moment! A colleague of my brother Bill, who knew we were traveling to China, had mailed the letter a month earlier. This dear lady planned to leave the city the next morning, so we were all astounded by God's supernatural timing.

I was invited to share about our heart for China and what the Lord was calling us to do to encourage our Chinese brothers and sisters in their work of spreading the Gospel in their land. When the meeting was over, they took me to yet another gathering to share the same message with those believers.

Against all conventional wisdom, we blitzed the city with whatever literature we had left. I can think of no other spiritual experience in my life more potent than that evening. Peggy and I walked through the crowded, dimly lit streets, softly singing hymns and choruses as we smiled at people and gave them Gospels. The extraordinary power of God and the sense of His leading cemented our vision for China.

That first trip to China was significant for Peggy and me

for another more personal reason: It was funded by my mother, who by this time was in her seventies. Thirty years earlier, Mom had sent her son to Korea to fight against the Chinese. This time, she sent him to the Chinese with a message of forgiveness, hope, and love that could only be found in the Gospel of Christ. About six months after Peggy and I returned from China, Mom went home to be with her Lord—full of life and service right up to the end.

The door to China still seemed closed, but God started answering our prayers to find the "window" into this needy country. Mr. Cheng from the Chinese Embassy in Washington arranged for us to send a group of English teachers to the People's University in Beijing for the summer. It was a wonderful opportunity at the leading Marxist institution in the country, but we had no teachers and no one to lead them.

Right in the midst of wondering what we were going to do, I received a phone call from Dr. Lee Bruckner, who was head of the cross-cultural department at Liberty University. Lee and his wife, Dr. Lila, had served as missionaries to Afghanistan and also had a long-standing interest in China. He had heard about our desire to send a summer team to China, so he called to introduce himself.

Lee and Lila ended up leading our first summer team to China in 1982 and led a team there every summer for the next eight years. Lee has also been a member of our board of directors since then. Now in his seventies, he still works with us, opening new fields and traveling like a man in his twenties. We often joke that it's difficult to find a spot on the globe where he hasn't already been, since his well-worn passport shows stamps from scores of countries. We can truly say of him what Paul said of Timothy: "Our brother and God's fellow worker in spreading the gospel of Christ" (1 Thessalonians 3:2 NIV).

Peggy organized that summer team in 1982, as she had organized each of the summer teams since the first one in 1979, and it became virtually a full-time, year-round job for her. By the year 2000, we had helped to mobilize several thousand summer missionaries and short-term volunteers to serve alongside full-time workers all around the globe. God subsequently called many of these short-term workers to full-time missionary service.

As the Lord continued to link us up with the right people, it certainly helped that we were based in Washington, D.C., an international city where diplomats and dignitaries regularly passed through. The world was at our doorstep. One of the events we looked forward to each year was the National Prayer Breakfast, a significant Christian gathering that draws believers from across the country and around the world. The president of the United States always attends, and organizers also invite ambassadors and other international leaders of many different faiths who serve in the nation's capital.

You never knew who might sit at your table. At the 1982 breakfast, Peggy and I were surprised to be seated with the Chinese ambassador to the United States. Another year, we saw our friend Sir Peter Kenilorea, prime minister of the Solomon Islands, whom we had met a few years earlier when we took our first survey trip to his country. We invited the prime minister to our home for dinner, and the Secret Service agreed to provide the security—after a complete check of the house and external surroundings.

I wonder what our neighbors thought when a parade of black limousines and Secret Service agents turned onto our street, blocking it at both ends. The prime minister joined us as we feasted on a wonderful turkey dinner and enjoyed

Christian fellowship. There was plenty of food, so Peggy asked the Secret Service man in charge if he and his agents would like to come inside and join us. Suddenly the walkie-talkies started buzzing and agents seemed to appear out of nowhere to enjoy Peggy's great cooking.

The mission grew, and in 1982 we held our first official Candidate Orientation Program, attended by nineteen prospective missionaries who eventually served in Asia, Africa, and the South Pacific. Each year, the number seemed to rise, and by 1986, we had twenty-six candidates at Candidate Orientation, fifty summer missionaries, fifty-one U.S. members, and more than 100 national workers in seven countries. We also had a growing team of volunteers, supporters, and prayer partners. We had survived the day of small beginnings, and it was now time to step into the future.

CHAPTER 7

To the Regions Beyond

Our hope is that...we can preach the gospel in the regions beyond you. For we do not want to boast about work already done in another man's territory.

—2 Corinthians 10:15-16 (NIV)

It is then only reasonable to seek the work where the need is most abundant and the workers are fewest.

—James Gilmore, missionary to Mongolia (1872-93)

"There are no other missions that will send us to Mongolia. Will you, Mr. Fletcher?"

The young couple standing before me explained that they had a deep burden for Mongolia, but every mission agency they spoke with told them there was no way they could go there because the country was "closed." At that time, Mongolia was one of the most restricted countries in the world, but this couple felt the Lord calling them there.

We encouraged them that God had an "open window" and helped them put together a team of like-hearted new missionaries. While they waited for the window to open to Mongolia, they went to Budapest, Hungary, where one of the universities had a visiting professor from a university in Mongolia. It was the best place to start learning the Mongolian language—even though they had to use an old language book written in Czechoslovakian to do so!

In 1989, when the Iron Curtain fell, there was only a handful of believers in all of Mongolia—possibly as few as ten. Our team was among the very first foreign missionaries to enter the country. It certainly helped that they already knew some of the language, and God used them to win and disciple Mongolians.

A few years later, this same couple prayed, "Lord, You've raised up so many missionaries here now. Where else do You need us?" They felt the Lord calling them to Libya—a country that seemed completely closed at the time, but that only made the need to go all the greater. They spent the next few years working with Libyans elsewhere in the Middle East and are still praying for the door to open for them to reside in Libya. They are the epitome of pioneers; they just won't give up!

There were more young people like this couple who were ready to go wherever the Lord called them—and Peggy and I didn't want to turn away any of them. We didn't want a single potential missionary to conclude, "I can't go there." That's why we decided from the start to *recruit for quantity, and screen for quality.* We knew that a lot of young people who talked with mission agencies were exploring God's will for their lives, and when they came to us, we wanted to be sensitive to where they were and not rule them out immediately for reasons that were not biblical. There will always be some applicants who "don't make it" for any one of a thousand reasons, but we wanted to cast the net very wide. We took every inquiry seriously and encouraged each person as much as possible. The application procedure itself is a natural screening process—filling out forms, being interviewed, taking a Bible test, undergoing psychological testing, and more. Furthermore, we work with applicants in partnership with their local churches, and send out only those who have been fully endorsed by a home sending fellowship. The entire process allows plenty of time to look at someone's calling, training, gifts, personality, temperament, aptitude, interests, ministry values, and more. We knew applicants would hear from God during that time, as would we.

Many of our first recruits came from Washington Bible College, and later from Columbia Bible College and Seminary in South Carolina, one of the top mission schools in the country. Two of our children had become students at Columbia, and because they were headed for the mission field, they knew everyone else on campus who was, too. Many of the 1,000 students enrolled there wanted to go into missions full-time. When Peggy and I made recruiting trips to the college, they approached our display booth in the student center and asked about possibilities for reaching the unreached areas of the world.

Instinctively, I began saying things to them that I wished people had said to us when we applied to be missionaries twenty years earlier: "So you want to be a missionary? Great! It's no problem that you don't have all your training yet. We'll work with you and your church to get that taken care of, and before you know it you'll be out on the field. The harvest is plentiful but the laborers are few. Be one of the few! We've been praying for people just like you who are willing to forsake all and follow Christ."

I liked the can-do attitude of Rick Clark, who was our director of mobilization. He would say to students, "Don't let anybody tell you that you can't get into India. India is wide open to the Gospel and we can get you there."

Many of the young people we met back in those days are

still serving on the mission field with PIONEERS today. One student we met, for example, told us after her summer trip to China, "I *have to* get back to China." There was a sense of urgency in her words, as if she really understood the monumental size of the harvest field in that country. We had an open door there, so we were able to send her right away. She is still in China, now with her husband and children.

Another student we met at Columbia was a young man named Steve Richardson. Steve grew up in Irian Jaya, Indonesia, where his parents were missionaries. His father, Don Richardson, wrote the classic mission books *Peace Child*, *Lords of the Earth*, and *Eternity in Their Hearts*. Steve was one of the mission "visionaries" on Columbia's campus. President of the Student Mission Fellowship, he had a passion for the unreached Sundanese Muslim people on the island of Java in Indonesia. At the time, they were considered the largest unreached people group in the world, numbering 33 million.

Our board had been praying about launching a new outreach to the Sundanese, so it was a natural match. Steve put his administrative and leadership gifts to work and built a team to match the task—including our daughter Arlene, whom he married in 1983. Within a few years, Steve and Arlene helped to assemble a team of forty enthusiastic missionaries. Among them were our daughter Carol, and her husband, Gary Franz. It was our largest team at the time.[5]

The team initiated an array of creative ministries including English schools, literature publication, relief work, and theological training for national workers. Arlene started a self-help program called Agape Craft, which today employs 200 local workers who make and sell quilts, wooden crafts, stuffed toys, and other items. Not only does Agape Craft provide jobs and training for the unemployed, but it is also an excellent witness of how Christians can apply godly principles to business endeavors. One of the other members of this team, John Fain, was involved in a theological school that trained national workers. Many years later, John became our director of international ministries.

From that Sundanese Team have come additional teams that are now bringing the Good News to other unreached groups in Indonesia, many also numbering in the millions.

As our staff on the field grew, our headquarters staff grew as well. God would bring us people in the most remarkable ways. For example, Barb Snyder, from York, Pennsylvania, where my brother Harry was a pastor, heard about an opening for a job as my secretary. While I was interviewing her, we needed to send out some receipts, and since there was no one else to help, I asked Barb if she wouldn't mind typing them. That was in December 1984, and Barb has been with us ever since. She came to us without promise of support and just trusted the Lord to provide for her. She is the equal of the finest secretaries I worked with in the business world and also became like another daughter to Peggy and me.

Other key staff came at a time when we were expanding and needing the right people. One of them was Jerry Knisley, our first full-time accountant. Jerry and his wife, Mary, were a great blessing to us, and we felt a tremendous loss when the Lord called Jerry home a few years later after a long battle with cancer.

God sent us more and more young people who wanted to blaze new paths to the unreached. In fact, we decided to change our name to describe more accurately the call that the Lord had given us. We also needed a name that would be more "security" sensitive—one that didn't sound like a Christian mission so that we could protect our missionaries in restricted-access countries. I remembered hearing that only one out of every ten missionaries is pioneering on new frontiers. We wanted a mission in which ten out of ten were pioneering, so we chose the new name "PIONEERS" to reflect our desire not to follow the worn paths, but to blaze new ones.

Our board also defined our focus of ministry. At the time, there were thousands of unreached people groups around the world, so we asked the Lord on which groups within the six unreached blocks did He want us to focus our efforts. We felt He directed us to these unreached peoples: the Kurds in Turkey (part of the Muslim block); the Fulani in Mali, West Africa (Muslim block); the urban Buddhists in Bangkok (Buddhist block); the Hindus and Muslims in Mauritius; the Sundanese in Indonesia (Muslim), and the Pokot in Kenya (Tribal). One of these groups, the Fulani, was considered so difficult to reach that one mission had pulled out their workers. After forty years of missions work there, they had two converts; one was killed and the other disappeared. We were sobered by the task ahead of us, but not overwhelmed. If God would help us to raise up a team, we determined to focus on those with the least opportunity to hear, regardless of how dangerous or how difficult the task might be.

Armed with a new name and a defined focus, we began aggressively recruiting a new breed of missionaries who were looking for a pioneering approach to reaching the unreached. We moved forward by faith and trusted that God would open doors and windows, and give us the strategies we needed.

As God sent young people our way—first baby boomers, and then baby busters after them—we saw them as a unique force for world evangelization. These teenagers and young adults thought about their faith and life in more relational terms. We were drawn to them, and they to us. In time, the Lord also attracted older, second-career missionaries to us, who were young at heart and full of zeal.

They all liked our flexible approach and what we today call our core values. Our number one core value is a passion for God. In everything we do, our heart is to glorify God among the nations. Two, we focus on unreached peoples. There are many good mission boards doing excellent work, but we don't want to duplicate what they are doing. Our maxim is, "Do not go where the path may lead; go where there is no path and leave a trail." We want to go to those who have never had an opportunity to hear the Gospel, and that means focusing on peoples with the greatest need and least opportunity to hear and understand the Gospel.

Three, we work in partnership with the local church—the key to sending as well as receiving missionaries. We stress to our missionaries that they need to have a strong relationship with their home church as their "senders." Once on the field, we partner with local national churches and ministries (where they already exist) to accomplish the task. Four, we initiate church-planting movements, resulting in dynamic, self-perpetuating and multiplying churches that also have a missionary vision so that they, too, become missionary-sending churches.

Five, we're team centered, and accomplish our mission through teams of people who use all their combined gifts to get the job done. Six, we believe in participatory servant-leadership. Our team leaders are there to serve the people under them. That's why we base our area directors on the field (unlike some mission agencies who base their field leadership in the home office).

Seven, we try to use innovative approaches to reach and minister to unreached peoples. Most of the countries we work in don't welcome missionaries, so we look for outside-the-box creativity to get our teams to these places. One important way is through bi-vocational workers—doctors, nurses, builders, engineers, teachers, administrators, and business people. They have legitimate non-religious jobs that grant them work visas, but their primary purpose is to make Christ known and, however possible, work toward starting a church. Today, about seventy percent of our missionaries are bi-vocational workers, otherwise known as "tentmakers."

Finally, we believe in the ethos of grace, meaning that God's grace operates uniquely in the lives of all believers, enhancing our personal and cultural diversity. In all our relationships, we try to cultivate an atmosphere of mutual acceptance, which encourages each of us to attain our full potential in Christ. Our Statement of Faith affirms all essential evangelical doctrines while leaving secondary, less consequential issues as matters of personal position. As a result, we have a broad-based membership and partnership, which we think accurately reflects the heart of the Gospel and the mind of Christ.

Some of these core values must have appeared radical at the time, and not surprisingly, caused some concern. For example, when we applied to join the Interdenominational Foreign Mission Association (IFMA), a national association of more than 100 mission boards, our reception from some of the members was, frankly, less than enthusiastic. We had been encouraged to pursue membership so that we could network with others and learn from them, which we were pleased to do. When we met with the board, however, the leadership of some of the older, established mission agencies seemed to view us as the "new kids on the block" who for various reasons were encroaching on their territory. One leader looked at our brochure that mentioned a people group in east Africa to whom we were hoping to minister. He bluntly told me, "We have been working with this people group." Although that was true, nonetheless, there were 180,000 still totally unreached people, and no one was working with them. He and others insinuated that we were being competitive, and they implied that our entering the scene was not "constructive" to the unity of their fraternity.

Others didn't like the "distinctives" mentioned in our brochure, which they felt were arrogant. For example, we emphasized a "simplified lifestyle" for our missionaries, a team approach to working on the field, and a policy that left decisions up to parents regarding the education of their children. At the time, most missions required that missionaries send their children to mission boarding schools, but we felt if parents wanted to keep their children with them and rely on home schooling, it was their prerogative.

We also came under fire for stressing what we called "personal sensitivity" to the needs of the individual missionary—trying to follow a flexible approach to each situation. To us, it made more sense to accommodate our policies to our missionaries so that they could achieve their greatest potential, rather than expecting our missionaries to accommodate themselves to our policies. We believed (and still do) that this would result in a higher morale for them and a better relationship with mission leadership.

We also developed our own policy on furloughs, which we felt was more flexible. At the time, most missions required missionaries to work on the field a set number of years before taking their home assignment (furlough). We felt it should be up to the individual missionary in consultation with their team leader and home sending church. Some people can go five years without going home, while others, particularly single missionaries and those working in difficult situations, might need more frequent and shorter breaks.

Still others felt we shouldn't send young people to the field to start new teams; they said missionaries, especially the leaders, needed to be experienced. It always amazed me that as a country we didn't think twice about sending teenagers to war, but apparently sending them into spiritual battle was a different matter.

The reaction we received from our peers in those early days was mystifying, and it could also have been discouraging had the Lord not sent key people to stand with us. Among them was Dr. Robert Alderman, who was our chairman of the board. Bob was a stabilizing force, someone who could balance vision with the structures and policies needed to support it. I'm sure many of my responses to these mission leaders may have seemed naïve, with a "corporate" edge to them, but Bob was able to guide us through the meetings. He saw beyond my weaknesses and genuinely wanted to be part of building our mission into a godly and credible movement.

Bob earned his doctorate in ministry from Trinity Evangelical Divinity School and wrote his dissertation on church/mission relationships. As pastor of Shenandoah Baptist Church in Roanoke, Virginia, he emphasized our need to nurture strong partnerships with local sending churches. Bob's heartbeat, and ours, was that the local church should be actively involved in the sending process. Many local churches simply delegated foreign missions to their denomination's mission board, but we felt that a missionary should be sent by his or her local church, not by the mission board. This process would involve the local church not only supporting its missionary but also making important decisions affecting his or her ministry, thus giving the church joint ownership of the work being done on the field. I met Bob during a strategic time at PIONEERS when we were experiencing internal growing pains. He moved into a place of leadership on our board and emerged as the spokesman. Bob was a real defender for us and what we stood for.

Among the other "encouragers" whom the Lord sent us were Dr. Edwin L. (Jack) Frizen, Jr., who was executive director of IFMA, and his wife, Grace. It was Jack who encouraged us to apply for membership in IFMA, and he upheld our merits to the board, which did finally accept us as full members. The Frizens seemed to recognize that Peggy and I were going against the tide, but saw a genuineness in our spirits and a readiness to get on with the task of world evangelization. They could see that our pioneering effort flowed with the stream of missions history and God's continued pursuit of the lost, the least, and the forgotten.

God used the challenges that we faced in those days to clarify who we were and where He was calling us. Someone once said, "Trials are just trails to the overcomer." Opposition showed us that we were blazing new paths and didn't fit into the mainstream mold. God continued to bring us qualified, dynamic people who didn't fit the mold, either—people who were willing to risk their all for Him, pioneers who wouldn't quit, and who wouldn't do things the old way just because "that's how we've always done it."

Right behind these baby boomers were the baby busters—and behind them the Gen Xers, the Millennials, and the Gen Yers. We realized that to effectively mobilize the missionary force of the next generation, we have to observe the current teenage culture because they're the ones we will be recruiting in seven to ten years—and they will always be different from our current missionaries. What was "cutting edge" to the baby boomers seems dull and rusty to the next generation. We must be willing to change and adapt, to allow each generation the opportunity to own the vision and move forward without being weighed down by the past.

No matter how effective and innovative we've been in the past, we have to remain pioneers—or we'll be in danger of becoming like the people who thought Peggy and I were "misguided radicals." A new breed is always just around the corner!

CHAPTER 8

It Takes a Team

By this all men will know that you are my disciples, if
you love one another.
>   —John 13:35 (NIV)

If you want to go fast, go alone. If you want to go far,
go together.
>   —African proverb

The drive to Williamsburg, Virginia, was particularly
meaningful on this day in February 1986. A day earlier, I had
spoken at a mission conference at Appalachian Bible College
in West Virginia, and Peggy and I were now enjoying the drive
through rural Virginia with our daughter and son-in-law,
Arlene and Steve Richardson. As we passed through
Richmond, near places where we used to live when I was with
Mobil, we had such a sense of God leading us by His hand
over the past quarter century.

When we arrived at our friends' home in Williamsburg,
Peggy and Arlene headed out to do some shopping, while

Steve and I tackled the long overdue revision of PIONEERS policy handbook. While we were working, I started to experience some discomfort in my chest. I tried to shrug it off at first, thinking it was indigestion, but the pain just increased. Suddenly, I felt as if I were going to be sick, so I ran up the stairs to the bathroom—probably the worst thing I could have done. By this time, I could barely breathe and felt as if my chest was caving in.

Steve called an ambulance, and I was rushed to the hospital. The diagnosis was a massive heart attack. When Peggy arrived, I was lying on my back and hooked up to oxygen tubes. It was ten days before I left the hospital, and another three months before I could even leave our home and go to the office to do some light work. My family realized more than I did what was going on. They knew I was overworked and didn't know how to pace myself.

It wasn't since Korea that I had come so close to death and been so humbled by the frailty of my own mortality. Slowly I recovered—due to God's grace, Peggy's care, and the prayers of many friends around the world. On a trip to China in the summer of 1987, I even climbed the Great Wall again. It seemed as if my health problems might be behind me, but the following April I had another heart attack. I knew it was time for me to slow down and let someone else guide PIONEERS. I tendered my resignation as general director, to be effective as soon as a replacement could be found, which I urged the board to do within six months.

Our board chairman, Bob Alderman, asked for my recommendations for someone to take my place. I replied that we had a lot of qualified young people to choose from, but they all seemed to be established in their ministries, so we might have to look outside the mission.

Bob asked permission to contact my son, John, to see if he

would consider the position. Of course I said that was fine, but added that John would probably say "no." By now he and his wife, Celia, were living in a remote jungle in Papua New Guinea as missionaries to the Kubo, an unreached tribe of 550 people. John had felt a call to tribal work since he was a teenager, and he and Celia had long-range plans to translate the New Testament. We all knew this was their heart and we couldn't see them leaving Papua New Guinea.

Yet, as the board met to discuss my replacement, there was a strong sense of the presence of God, and the unmistakable impression that His hand was on John's life. God's leading was so clear, in fact, that the board immediately voted to offer John the position. He was just 29 years old at the time, but to everyone, including me, it was obvious that PIONEERS needed his administrative gifts and vision to take the mission forward.

To John and Celia, the offer initially made no sense at all, yet they also were overwhelmed by God's leading. John remembers walking up and down the airstrip that he had helped to carve out of the jungle, pondering the board's offer and praying for God's direction. While their work with the Kubo was not yet complete, they knew that God could raise up someone else to take over and see it to completion. He and Celia knew God was calling, and so by the summer of 1988, they had traded the jungles of Papua New Guinea for the fast-paced life of the Washington, D.C., area.

John certainly had his work cut out for him. For the first time in PIONEERS existence, we had a cash flow deficit in our general fund. The $90,000 deficit might as well have been $9 million to us. The figure seemed astronomical, with no hope in sight to bring it down. We had always paid our bills on time, but suddenly we felt paralyzed by a balance sheet that seemed to threaten our ability to grow and expand.

John's first tasks were eliminating the debt and finding

creative ways to cut back on operating expenses. God's provision came through my good friend, Jim Ryan, founder of Ryland Homes, who offered a matching grant through the Ryan Family Foundation. He originally offered it with the stipulation that I retire because he was concerned about my health, but I felt that would not be consistent with God's call on my life. Jim reconsidered but held firm to another stipulation: The funds had to be raised within three weeks. John immediately sent out a special appeal letter inviting our supporters to give. All the money came in, plus some. Together with the Ryan match, we raised $100,000—and by the grace of God, we were out of debt. Jim has been a wonderful friend time and again to this mission and to me personally. The Lord used him in many ways to strengthen and encourage me at critical times in my life.

In August, I had a third heart attack, but it was mild compared to the other two. Still, it showed me the need to maintain the regime the Lord put me on and not take on too much in my zeal to reach the unreached. When Jim McCracken, our director of personnel, left to launch our Turkey Team, John offered me Jim's position. He knew I'd love my new assignment: recruiting missionaries. I *did* love it. It really took me back to the basics and to our early days, and I had a wonderful time talking with young people and fanning the mission flames that God had ignited inside them. God brought a record fifty-eight prospective missionaries to our June 1989 Candidate Orientation. The most we had ever had was twenty-two, so we felt He was saying our future was bright.

God wasn't finished restructuring PIONEERS just yet, however. We already knew the importance of teams and teamwork on the field. Now, He started showing us they were important in our home office and the board room, too. In 1989, John had met a British missionary named Bob Hitching, and the two hit it off immediately. I hadn't met Bob yet, but John assured me he was our kind of guy—a real pioneer for the Lord. He had been imprisoned for the Gospel in Turkey while serving with Operation Mobilization, and had a strong interest in a Muslim people group in eastern Europe that hardly anyone had heard of at the time—the Bosnians.

Like many creative people, Bob is a night owl, and would call John at all hours with ideas and inspiration. One night, he called John at 10:30 p.m. and asked if they could meet. Bob was an hour-and-a-half away, but drove over to meet with John. He got right to the point asking one of his no-nonsense questions: "How are you going to grow this mission?"

John gave some faith-filled response such as, "We're going to trust God," to which Bob replied, "Then you're going to die doing it." At the time, our twelve team leaders reported directly to John. That was fine when we were a small mission with three or four leaders, but Bob knew PIONEERS had the potential to grow much bigger. He told John he would need to develop a new structure of leadership to manage that growth, or he'd be the next one to have a heart attack from stress.

That late-night meeting led to others, and John, Bob Hitching, and our son-in-law Gary Franz, who had returned from the field in Indonesia to become our director of personnel, identified key areas of the world where PIONEERS was working. In each area, they selected key leaders, who became our area directors—and our first International Leadership Team.

Bob's emphasis on Eastern Europe was the hand of God directing us to blaze a path in a newly opened area, and within five years, PIONEERS placed nearly seventy workers in that region. Only God knew how strategic that area would become in a few years, and He made sure we had people in place, ready to serve. Eventually, Bob became chairman of our board and helped expand our borders even further. Just as importantly, he became to John what friends like Bob Alderman, Phil Steyne, Lee Bruckner, AC Levi, and Ken Clary had been to me in the early years: gifts from the Lord who would offer encouragement, wisdom, and counsel, and keep us accountable along the way.

As God continued building our team on the field and in the board room, we fine-tuned our mission statement with nineteen words that summed up our calling and focus: "PIONEERS mobilizes teams to glorify God among unreached peoples by initiating church-planting movements in partnership with local churches."

From Mongolia to Mali, PIONEERS was rapidly expanding with teams all over the world. Here are a few snapshots from our China, Indonesia, and North Korea Teams.

China: Scaling the Great Wall

Back in 1979 when Harry Liu and I went to the Chinese Embassy to "make friends," the wall around that country did seem high and, indeed, great. How would more than one billion Chinese hear about the Lord Jesus? How would people groups such as the Tibetans, Mongols, Uygurs, Buyi, and others ever know His love—peoples who spoke their own languages and had their own unique cultures?

We knew it would take teamwork to get the job done. Our work in China started with a team of two English teachers, whom we recruited in response to Mr. Cheng's invitation. That team eventually grew to 52 adults, who today reach out to unreached people groups all over the country.

To make sure our teams are as well cared for as possible,

we have team leaders whose responsibility is to oversee and encourage their fellow team members. Our China Team, for example, is so large that we have several teams and team leaders, as well as a support link outside the mainland to help them—PIONEERS missionary Elizabeth Stockton (not her real name). Elizabeth lives elsewhere in East Asia and regularly travels inside China to encourage and help her teammates. Outside China, she serves them by coordinating plane tickets, making doctor and dental appointments, receiving and passing on mail, making airport pickups, acting as communications liaison between China and the world (including our headquarters), and more. Many outsiders have told Elizabeth that they're blessed by our team relationships and concern for one another.

For teams working in countries such as China, team unity can speak volumes. A few years ago, some of our team members invited fifteen Chinese friends to spend the night before Easter in their home. The group stayed up late, talking until the early hours of the morning. They listened to a tape about a Chinese intellectual who was searching for God, followed by a discussion that kept the workers on their toes. At 3:00 in the morning, everyone headed to the Great Wall for a sunrise service and celebration. One of the unbelievers said, "I am like a child who has only known the color red, and now, for the first time, I am discovering there are other colors out there."

One out of every five people on our planet today is Chinese. What will we do to reach them? There are hundreds of people groups in China, and most still know "only the color red." There is a high and great wall around them, but the love of Christ as modeled by our team members is slowly causing that wall to crumble. Psalm 18:29 promises, "With my God I can scale a wall" (NIV). We continue to believe that no country is too closed—and no wall too impenetrable—for the Lord.

Indonesia: Islands of Unreached

A number of years ago, a young woman I'll call Melissa read an article by a PIONEERS missionary describing one of Indonesia's unreached groups, the Nabea (not their real name). The 70,000 Nabeas are Muslim and live on a small island that has more than 300 mosques. The island where the Nabeas live is called the Isle of Women because many of the men leave their homes to work in Singapore and elsewhere, returning to the island only to die. There has been no Gospel witness among this people group, partly because anyone who opposes Islam or converts to Christianity will be killed.

As Melissa prayed for the Nabea people, the Lord said to her, "You're asking Me to save these people. Will you be My instrument to accomplish it?"

Melissa responded to the call and joined one of our teams. She visited the island, built relationships, learned the language, and shared her faith. Today there is at least one Nabea Christian. Another family has joined Melissa, and we now have a team working to plant a church among this group.

But what of the other 130 unreached people groups in this country, representing tens of millions of people, living on hundreds of scattered islands? Many of them are Muslim (Indonesia is world's most populous Muslim country); others are Hindu (the island of Bali alone has 46,000 temples) or animist. They are all disillusioned and desperate—no wonder, in the face of terrible social, religious, political, and economic crises of recent years.

Back in the 1980s, Craig and Elaine Stevenson (not their real names) began praying for one of these unreached groups—the 33 million Konahare Muslims (name changed for security reasons). In the past, missionaries had made scattered attempts to proclaim the Gospel among the Konahare but without much success. Today most Konahare have still never heard the Gospel. To them, to be a Konahare is to be Muslim.

As Craig and Elaine, along with friends at their Bible college, asked God to open a door for the Konahare to hear the Good News, they decided to become the answer to their own prayers. They formed a PIONEERS team to take the Good News to them. When they arrived in Indonesia, they immersed themselves in densely populated urban communities, and in time learned both the national language and the Konahare language. They studied the history and linked with local Christians who were also burdened to reach the Konahare, praying for a strategy to reach the people.

Team members Tom and Nancy O'Hara (not their real names) developed a ministry strategy they called "Lampstand," based on Matthew 5:15-16: "Neither do people light a lamp and put it under a bowl. Instead they put it on its stand, and it gives light to everyone in the house. In the same way, let your light shine before men, that they may see your good deeds and praise your Father in heaven" (NIV).

The team's goal was to take the Gospel out of "hiding" so that 33 million Konahare would hear and understand it. They focused on two levels of ministry: sharing the Gospel with Muslim neighbors and friends, and launching strategic ministries that would ultimately strengthen the growing Konahare Christian community.

Today, our team has helped to plant about ten churches, published the Bible in the Konahare language, trained national evangelists, started a church-planting coordination center, and launched a number of creative community development programs and English schools. They have also produced Gospel tracts, discipleship materials, radio programs, teaching tapes, and the first and only Christian publication in the Konahare language, an evangelistic magazine with a circulation of 10,000.

This team, which includes members from many countries (including Indonesia), works closely with national churches and other agencies, and also partners with their sending churches, who play an important role in what God is doing in Indonesia—churches such as Grace Fellowship in Baltimore, Church of the Saviour in Wayne, Pennsylvania, and Cherrydale Baptist in Arlington, Virginia.

Through this partnership, the lives of many Konahare are being changed. Mahmud, for example, was a milk delivery boy when he first accepted Christ. He has now been to Bible school and is pastoring a growing Konahare congregation. He and other believers published a Konahare hymnbook and taught people to worship using traditional instruments.

All these tools are helping to shine the light of the Gospel to even more Konahare. In fact, at a recent gathering of 640 Konahare believers, sixteen guests placed their faith in Christ. The next day, irate Muslims threw stones at the meeting place, so the growing Konahare Christian community has not gone unnoticed.

The Konahare is one of the largest and least reached people groups in the world, and just one example of what the Lord is doing in Indonesia. PIONEERS Indonesia field includes eighty-three people working among fifteen of the country's largest unreached groups. Using "creative access" approaches, they serve as teachers, consultants, students, and business people, all with the goal of establishing strong, reproducing churches.

As Isaiah prophesied, "The islands will look to me and wait in hope for my arm" (Isaiah 51:5 NIV).

North Korea: Of Rice and Rifles

God first stirred my heart for the nations fifty years ago when I served with the Marine Corps on the Korean peninsula. There, I gave my life to the Lord. I was free to do so, but today millions of North Koreans would face death for making the same decision. The communist dictatorship of

North Korea is perhaps the tightest in the world. The totalitarian government demands blind allegiance and even worship of former leader Kim Il Sung, who bankrupted the country before he died in the late 1990s. His legacy lives on through his son, Kim Jong Il, and their pictures hang in every home and over every heart—while the people eat whatever they can to survive.

Experts believe that 100,000 Christians are among the millions of prisoners in the country's labor camps, where they face starvation, torture, and murder. A government dictionary defines a church as "an organization that spreads poisonous anti-government ideas to take people's rights away, disguised as religious activity."[6] What a contrast to the early twentieth century when the capital, Pyongyang, had so many churches that it was known as the "Jerusalem of the East."

Since 1994, our North Korea Team, located elsewhere in East Asia, has been praying and preparing for the day when the door opens to this repressed country. They have been learning the language and waiting for visa opportunities to gain permanent residency. Meanwhile, they do what they can to serve North Koreans who risk their lives to escape across the border into neighboring countries. The home church of one team member donated funds to buy rice. Team members distributed the food to starving refugees, and also shared the Gospel with them—and many have come to know Christ.

Despite extreme oppression by the communist regime, the Christian church has grown inside North Korea, slowly and silently. Could God be preparing a great spiritual harvest there as He has in China and other restricted countries?

North Korea, Indonesia, China—we continue to believe that a country cannot be "closed" to the Lord. Around the world, PIONEERS teams pray and prepare for the day when God will open the doors to the countries that He has laid on their hearts.

CHAPTER 9

A Time to Build

There is a time for everything...a time to build.
—Ecclesiastes 3:1, 3 (NIV)

Never tell people how to do things. Tell them what to
do and they will surprise you with their ingenuity.
—General George Patton

When Jesus told Peter that the gates of hell would not
overcome His church, I think He must have been warning
Peter what he was going to face as an early church planter in
the first part of the first millennium—building and over-
coming.

That certainly describes what we faced during the final
part of the second millennium—an era of great expansion as
well as tremendous battle. By God's grace, PIONEERS grew
faster and farther than we ever dreamed. In 1994, we were
identified as the fastest-growing mission in the Interdenominational Foreign Mission Association. We had grown to 360
missionaries and appointees and 141 international workers in
twenty-nine countries—amazing growth in just fifteen years.

God warns us in His Word that the enemy would come to
seek, kill, and destroy, but He also promises that the gates of

hell would not overcome His church. He has been faithful to His Word, helping us to fulfill the second part of our mission statement—to "initiate church-planting movements" wherever we work around the world.

In restricted-access countries where PIONEERS works, our missionaries can't just pass out fliers inviting people to attend a new church. They could be imprisoned or even killed—as could anyone who showed up for the meeting. Church planting can be a long process that begins with finding creative ways to enter these countries, learning the language and culture, and spending time to build relationships with the local people. That's why PIONEERS mobilizes missionaries who are commissioned by their sending churches to follow the New Testament pattern of establishing churches.

The first step in church planting is entering the country – and sometimes that takes creativity. Jeff and Cindy Warner from Groton Heights Baptist Church in Connecticut, for example, lived in Croatia learning the language and culture while waiting for the door to open to Bosnia. They launched an innovative sports ministry that led to the salvation of several young Croat teens. Jeff convinced the Croatian government to start a national Croatian softball team, which he and Cindy coached, and Jeff went on to become the Croatian commissioner of softball. It's not your usual mission strategy, but it works.

Once on the field, the next step toward planting a church is building relationships. Krista (not her real name) has been a part of PIONEERS team to the Balinese people in Indonesia. A single woman, Krista travels twice a month on her motorcycle to a remote mountain village to share stories from the Old Testament. The people have been very open to her ministry, and, against all odds she's helping to plant the seeds of the Gospel that will someday grow into a strong New Testament, mission-sending church.

Taking the time to build relationships is important to most cultures around the world, and it would be impossible to build a church without this key step. Two of our team members serving among Tibetans in Nepal, for example, say that the majority of their work is relational. "We act out the life and Gospel of Jesus through our friendships with Tibetans," they explain. "One of the many ways to begin friendships is to meet a felt need. The Tibetans we live among are refugees and have few job skills of practical use in this developing country."

This couple is helping Tibetans with language and job skills that will give them a competitive edge in the local job market. A few Buddhist monks even attend the husband's English class, and one of the graduates of the wife's cooking class has already opened her own bakery shop.

PIONEERS workers in other countries also use various means to build relationships, all with the end goal of church planting—"tea debates" among Muslims in West Africa, a "Let's Talk About Life" discussion group in Sarajevo, coffee shops in Hungary and Mongolia, a Mexican restaurant in Macedonia, men's gatherings in Kuwait, English-language programs, and many other creative means.

When a team finally plants a church, they have an entirely new to-do list as they encourage and mobilize national workers to "go" themselves, until all peoples hear the Gospel. By the grace of God, PIONEERS teams have planted churches in Macedonia, India, Kosovo, Lebanon, Benin, Kazakhstan, Indonesia, Papua New Guinea, Thailand, and elsewhere.

Eastern Europe: Planting Churches Amidst Rubble

In 1992 we added the "secular world" as the sixth block of unreached peoples that PIONEERS would focus on for church planting—peoples in eastern Europe and the countries that made up the former Soviet Union. People in this block may appear to be religious from a cultural standpoint, but in reality they are "practical atheists." A Croatian, for example, told one of our missionaries, "I'm Catholic, but I don't believe in God." For many people in the secular block, their family religious background is an integral part of their cultural identity, but they don't profess any belief in God. To them, religion is totally irrelevant to daily life. A large percent of Europeans believe in astrology, good luck charms, and fortune tellers, and animism in the form of magic continues to thrive on the continent.[7]

When the doors to Eastern Europe opened, the Lord helped us put together teams for Croatia, Bosnia, Albania, and Macedonia. Our area director for Europe, Mike Johnson, and his wife, Diana, lived in Croatia for eight years when it was still part of communist Yugoslavia. There, they started an indigenous church-planting mission and also founded the Yugoslav Bible Institute. However after several months of daily visits to the Zagreb police station for questioning, they knew their time in Croatia had come to an end.

The Johnsons relocated to Austria to work with a Bible school—and that's where Bob Hitching, who by this time had become our board chairman, caught up with them. Bob knew that Mike was a pioneer at heart and would never be happy unless he was blazing new paths and opening new fields. He told them about a need in Bosnia, and when Mike and Diana headed there in 1992, no one knew that war was about to break out. Mike put on a bulletproof vest and maneuvered his way through U.N. checkpoints into Sarajevo. Fluent in the language, he was able to get himself into the most war-torn regions of the country.

What he saw and heard was horrifying. More than

200,000 civilians had been killed, and 80,000 women and girls raped. Appalling as it sounds, rapists would attack Muslim women, gouge out their eyes, and then place wooden orthodox crosses on their dead bodies as a sign of their "Christian" victory over Islam. When Mike came back from those early trips, he mobilized and motivated his teams, who knew that God had given them an open door to share His love with 2 million Muslims who needed to hear it.

God began doing amazing things. Two of our couples who were already in Zagreb—the Warners, and Todd and Pamala Price—immediately headed for Zenica, a town of 300,000 that was forty percent Muslim before the war and eighty percent Muslim after the war. Through their personal witness and friendship, they planted a church within six months and later founded the Bosnian Bible Society.

Another team member, Rob Farnsley, from Fresno, California, moved to Mostar and promptly broke an old missions rule that people in their forties cannot learn foreign languages. Within a short period of time, Rob was preaching and teaching in the Bosnian language, and a church was planted in Novi Travnik.

Meanwhile, Ted and Nettie Esler, a young couple from Grace Church of Roseville, Minnesota, arrived in Sarajevo, where they helped to launch a comprehensive strategy that impacted Bosnian culture at several levels. It wasn't long before they helped to plant a church in the city, which was quickly handed over to national leadership. That church is now in the process of planting other churches in Sarajevo.

Still seeking to impact the entire culture, the team began strategizing and raising money for projects that would touch the entire country. One of the first was a playground, built in partnership with Kids Around The World, for the children of Dobrinja, the most heavily bombed part of Sarajevo. A playground may not seem like the most needed facility for a city recovering from war, but most of the local children had never played outside because there were so many land mines buried in the ground.

"Adventure Playground," which covers nearly half an acre, made an immediate impact on the city, and has opened doors for the Gospel in Sarajevo. In the days following the war, it was probably the only play area in Sarajevo, and was invariably crowded. On opening day alone, 30,000 children visited the site with their families!

The team came up with another creative idea to impact the community with the love of Jesus. They purchased a bombed-out building for a low price, removed about 70 tons of rubble, and turned it into an English-language institute, computer training center, and a facility where church members can be discipled in their new faith. Our niece, Mary Jo Fletcher, who was on the team at the time, played a strategic role during this foundational stage of the team's ministry.

One of their most far-reaching projects was arranging for the national TV stations to air two films in the Bosnian language: *Joni* and *The Hiding Place*. As a result, the largest number of Bosnians in history heard the Gospel of Christ at one time.

In neighboring Albania, our team has also planted a church, which helped to minister to many of the thousands of refugees from Kosovo who flooded into Albania during the war.[8] Most of the refugees were forced from their homes at gunpoint and fled with only the clothes on their backs. In Peshkopi, Albania, our team renovated a dormitory at a tech school to provide housing for 200 refugees. They invested $3,000 in painting, doors, windows, plumbing, electrical work, and more, and in the process, built relationships with the refugees. Peshkopi has known only Islam or Communism for five centuries, but in just a few years the Lord has raised up more than fifty believers. Three are in leadership training, and a new church is emerging. The team's goal is to purchase a building for a Christian center for worship services and also a school to teach English and computer skills. Unemployment in Peshkopi hovers above the fifty-percent mark, so a training school would stimulate the local economy and be a powerful evangelistic tool. Within the next four years, the team believes the Lord will direct them to move on to another town, allowing the Albanian believers to continue as an independent church—self-supporting, self-governing, and self-reproducing.

Kyrgyzstan: Starting From Ground Zero

One of the most exciting stories of church planting and God's redemptive power comes from the small land-locked country of Kyrgyzstan. In 1991, when the Soviet system fell apart and the Central Asia republics embraced independence, there were less than a dozen known believers among the Kyrgyz people and no known Kyrgyz fellowships. By the end of the twentieth century, there were more than 2,000 believers in forty-five churches, with an increasing number of well-trained, effective pastors.

Since 1994, PIONEERS has been a part of the partnership that God has raised up to grow His church in this country, which many believe will become a powerful force for missions and evangelism for the rest of Central Asia. PIONEERS workers in Kyrgyzstan are involved in discipleship, ethno-musicology, business development, and a number of other initiatives designed to empower national leaders to reach their own nation—including seemingly mundane events such as neighborhood cleanups. One Saturday evening, PIONEERS team members Kathy and Tom Sansera (not their real names) were working on their language study when there was a knock on their apartment door. One of their neighbors was inviting them to join the yearly clean-up of their apartment grounds— at 9:00 the next morning. Tom explained that they went to church on Sunday morning, so they wouldn't be able to help. The neighbor woman went away disappointed—and Tom and Kathy wondered if they had made the right decision. Wasn't God honored by their decision to testify to a stranger on His behalf, especially in this Muslim and secular nation? Then the Lord reminded them of the story of the Good Samaritan, and the Sanseras realized their decision would make them like the priest who hurried to his religious duties instead of helping a needy stranger.

The next morning, Tom ran down four flights of stairs to tell their neighbor that they had changed their minds. When she asked, "Why?" Tom had an opportunity to put his language study to good use. He shared the story about how a wounded Jewish traveler was helped by a despised Samaritan. The Kyrgyz woman listened intently to every word and then smiled. Tom and Kathy spent the morning picking up trash and sweeping the grounds with handmade brooms. By the time they finished, they had met every person in their apartment building. It wasn't the typical Sunday morning church service, but I believe God was very pleased with Tom and Kathy's decision. The friendships they made will surely help them reach their goal to plant a church in this Muslim country.

As part of our work in Kyrgyzstan, PIONEERS also focuses on the Dungan, an unreached people group that lives in the mountains and valleys of this beautiful country. About 44,600 Dungan live here—a proud people who are famous for their hospitality and hold many ceremonies and banquets to preserve their culture. Most Dungan are Muslim, and there are less than one percent Christians among them. Sixty percent have never even heard the Gospel. Our team's objective is to translate the New Testament and portions of the Old Testament into Dungan, promote literacy so that people can read the Scriptures, and plant churches in the four major Dungan towns.

All of this begins one relationship at a time, of course. A PIONEERS team member recently met one of the ten known Dungan believers, a young man we will call Sasha, who is studying at a local university. Sasha invited our team member to his village for a holiday celebration. "During the weekend," our team member told us, "Sasha, six of his male relatives, and I visited eight different Dungan homes in one day, eating and drinking tea at each home. They eat sweets first (pastries, candies) in one room, then move to another room and table where we were served meat, noodles, fish, bread, salad, pickles, and more. At one home, there was a twenty-foot table covered with five rows of bowls filled with pastries, raisins, nuts, cookies, and candies. I counted twenty-seven different kinds of candy!"

Sasha is undoubtedly the only believer in his family, and the holiday celebration included a visit to the local cemetery, where family members conducted religious rituals that showed our team member first-hand how lost the Dungan are without Jesus. Foreigners rarely get invited to such celebrations, and so the experience provided valuable relationship building that will eventually help plant a church among this people.

Mongolia: Building the True Kingdom

"I am so thankful to God that someone obeyed and came to my harvest field," a Mongolian Christian woman named Narangerel (not her real name) shared with PIONEERS team members. PIONEERS church-planting strategy is to involve national workers as much as possible, with the goal of giving them complete leadership and responsibility for the church. That day is coming in Mongolia, where just a decade ago you could count the number of Christians on two hands. Today there are probably 2,000 Christians in the country, including Narangerel, who shares her story:

> I was born and raised in Mongolia. When I grew up, there was not one church in my village of 20,000 people. Actually, there was not even one church in all of Mongolia. In 1990, God began to move. For the first time ever, the communist leaders allowed democratic elections. Mongolia opened to the western world.
>
> In the summer of 1992, a group of Korean Christians came to my village for a short time. There were only about ten people meeting at this time. When I returned from a year of working in another town, a friend showed me a New Testament and said that some people were going to the Jesus meeting. She handed me the New Testament, and I said, "What nice paper." I read the introduction and saw the name "Lord of the Universe." I thought, "Yes, I do believe that one God created everything. We didn't come from monkeys." That day was the first time I had ever heard the name Jesus. I had seen some movies and thought maybe Jesus was a Catholic priest.
>
> A few months later, another friend invited me to the Jesus meeting. There were about twenty to twenty-five people there. We sang some songs and a young Mongol man spoke about the Holy Spirit and Satan. I had heard about evil spirits before, but never about Satan. I certainly had never heard about the Holy Spirit.

After the meeting, some of us went to a believer's home to help him with some work. As we walked, they shared with me about Jesus and salvation. I didn't understand much, but on that day, October 4, 1992, I believed that Jesus had died for me and that I wanted to follow Him.

Since then, I have been a worker in my church leading the children's church. I became involved with PIONEERS when I helped the 1994 summer team conduct children's camps. I am a student at the Union Bible Training Center in Ulaanbaatar, Mongolia. My husband and I want to work in the countryside of Mongolia. Why? Because, like me a few years ago, too many people still don't know Jesus. It is difficult today to believe that people still have not heard. Jesus said to His disciples, "Pray for workers to go into the harvest fields. The harvest is plentiful, but the workers are few." I am so thankful to God that someone obeyed and came to my harvest field.

PIONEERS assisted in founding the Union Bible Training Center (UBTC), where Narangerel studied. The Center is an association of Mongolian churches and foreign ministries that work together to equip leaders for the emerging Mongol church. In three years, enrollment at UBTC grew from twenty-seven to 117 students. PIONEERS Mongolia Team leader served as director and later chairman of the board of the four-year school, which trains students academically and in practical situations where they put their "book knowledge" to work. Most students can't afford tuition, room, or board to attend the school, and their young churches can't contribute much to the costs, either. In fact, UBTC charges only fifteen percent of the actual cost to enable as many students as possible to attend. PIONEERS launched a scholarship program to reward students who attain high academic standing and spiritual development. This is a strategic way to affect the future of the Mongol church.

In 1994, Narangerel helped with a PIONEERS summer team working in Mongolia, and she met one of our American team members. They were married a few years later, and together hope to plant churches in remote areas of Mongolia.

Russia: From the Military to Missions

I wasn't the only one to draw on my military background when I stepped into missions. To launch our ministry in Russia, God used a retired U.S. Army lieutenant colonel named Warren Wagner. For two years before the collapse of the Soviet Union, Warren was stationed in Central Russia as a commander of the U.S. Missile Inspection Group. During that time, he developed relationships with Soviet officials, including those working in the Udmurt Republic. This area was the heart of the Soviet defense industry and was sealed off from the outside world during the communist era.

Warren retired from the military with a burden to reach the people he once worked with. His wife, Kim, already served in PIONEERS office in Sterling, Virginia, in the finance department, so when Warren retired, he joined PIONEERS.

It was the perfect match: We wanted to initiate a ministry in the former Soviet Union, and Warren had all the right contacts to do so. His relationships with former officials, combined with his vision for using innovative techniques, helped him to establish the Russian-American Christian Professionals Institute (RCPI) in Izhevsk. Today, this outreach includes business consultation, TV programming assistance, care for orphans, and classes in English, computers, and drama.

PIONEERS missionaries serve in partnership with national workers—Russians, Udmurts, Tatars, and other native peoples—to evangelize and plant churches in Izhevsk and the surrounding villages. God has raised up four new churches in the area, including a fledgling congregation in a village in Central Udmurtia. More than 100 people have already placed their faith in Christ and are working to show His love to others who are lost.

One of the first Udmurts whom our team reached out to was a seventeen year old named Andrei. Like any unsaved teenager, Andrei's main goal in life was having fun. On weekends, he would serve as a disk jocky for dances at his high school, and he had friends all over campus. Then he met a group of American English teachers—bi-vocational missionaries with PIONEERS who moved to his city in 1993 to minister with RCPI. Andrei was one of the first Udmurts that the team led to Christ. Today, he's still attracting a crowd—only now he talks about Jesus instead of rock and roll. He has a passion for evangelizing, discipling new believers, leading youth work, and taking a personal role in growing one of the strongest new churches in Izhevsk.

Middle East: A Voice in the Desert

As I write this book, I've just returned from a trip to the Middle East with my son, John. We traveled to Sudan, Egypt, and Lebanon to visit and encourage PIONEERS teams, hear their testimonies, and pray with them. Sudan is in the midst of the longest-running civil war on the planet. Since 1983, more than 2 million people have been killed and another million have starved to death because of famine. The radical Muslim government in the north has declared a jihad, or holy war, against the southern part of the country, populated by Christians and animists.

The team we partner with in Sudan serves in the midst of

extreme hardship and under constant threat of persecution. These twenty-five national workers and a handful of foreign Christians have a ministry of evangelism and church planting that includes outreach to refugee camps, a Christian bookstore, an orphanage, and a medical clinic. The war has displaced 4 million Sudanese, many of whom live in appalling conditions in refugee camps where there is little food or medical attention.

Words cannot describe the heart-wrenching conditions of these people who have not a hope in this world apart from Christ. We held two open-air evangelistic meetings in a camp on the outskirts of Khartoum, the capital city, which is located in the Muslim part of Sudan. Our team set up a stage and sound system on the sand, and more than 700 refugees listened as John preached about Abraham. John explained how the patriarch searched for the city that God had promised him, but lived in a tent all his life, only to discover that the city God promised was in Heaven. At the close of both meetings, many of these precious people trusted Christ for their salvation.

Helping to meet some of the needs of these believers is part of the way we assist them in church planting. In one refugee camp, where believers worship in the open air as temperatures soar past 100 degrees, we were asked to provide a new roof for the building, as well as benches and supplies for their one-room school. We supplied $10,000 worth of donated medicine for the team's medical clinic, which is strategically located in a major city. The clinic is a great help to the Muslim people in the area and provides an effective outreach to them.

Needless to say, life for team members in Sudan is not easy. One of the team doctors, a single man, lives in a simple room in the back of the clinic, and the national evangelists live on just $175 a month. Part of our goal in traveling to Sudan was to encourage these faithful workers. Each morning, John

Top: With Foodoo chief in
Benin, West Africa, 1999
Below: With Pokot tribesman
in Kenya near Ugandan
border, mid 1980s

With Peggy in Jordan, 1999

With Bedoin shepherds, Kuwait, after Gulf War

shared a devotional with the team, followed by moving testimonies from former Muslims who have been transformed by the Good News of salvation in Jesus Christ.

PIONEERS has teams in several other restricted-access countries in the Middle East, where they are praying and working to plant churches. In some countries, such as Kuwait, gaining ground for the Kingdom is a lengthy process. In other places, the church is growing dramatically. A PIONEERS couple in one very restricted country in the Middle East has seen some dramatic conversions. Judy, the wife, is an American, and her husband, Ali, is an Egyptian believer (not their real names). Their goal is to reach the 1.3 million Bedouins who live in the deserts of the Middle East. Most are unreached by the Gospel. Judy shares one of the exciting testimonies they've experienced:

> The man standing at our apartment door had all the indications of a very religious Muslim. I had never seen him before, but I did know the teenager with him—nineteen-year-old Tahir, who had accepted Christ just two days earlier.

> Tahir made the introductions: "This is my father, and he wants to talk to your husband...now."

> My husband, Ali, who is a Christian convert from Islam, had been working with Tahir for three months. Tahir was eager to learn and one of the most receptive people we've encountered. Earlier that week, Tahir had come to our apartment while we were meeting with Dr. Lee Bruckner, a member of PIONEERS board, and John Fain, who at the time was director of field ministries. They were in our country to find out first-

hand about our work and evaluate what type of workers would best assist us.

As they talked with Tahir, he made the life-changing decision to accept Christ and dedicate his life to Him. Ali had warned Tahir of the possible consequences of a Muslim embracing Christianity and even searched for a new job and living quarters for Tahir in another part of the country in case we needed to move him quickly.

All this was on my mind as I led Tahir and his father to the balcony to meet with Ali. Back in the kitchen preparing tea, I knew there could only be one reason for this unannounced visit. Within minutes, the secret police could arrive, if they were not already waiting downstairs. Tahir's father might even have planned for his other sons to murder Tahir. Killings like this had taken place in the past, and the convert's head would be placed on a pole for viewing. The local sheriff's report would state that it was an "accidental death."

Fear enveloped me. Silently I prayed, "Lord, anything is possible through You." Still the monster of fear gripped my throat. I told myself, "Faith the size of a mustard seed—surely you can do that."

Instantly my feelings melted into peace! I carried tea to the balcony and withdrew, watching the proceedings covertly. After half an hour, the father rose abruptly and left with Tahir. As soon as they were gone, I asked Ali what happened.

"Tahir told his father everything," Ali said. "He showed him his Bible and explained his conversion.

His father said Tahir had been a terror for years. He
had been disrespectful, cursed his parents, refused to
go to school, and did not want to work. He had van-
dalized the neighborhood and was a heartbreak to his
mother. Finally, his father threw him out of the house.
But he said for the last three months since I've been
working with Tahir, he has changed. He is diligent,
visits his parents often, and treats them with love and
respect. His father couldn't understand the change.
After Tahir told him he had been learning the Bible,
he began to understand."

I was in shock! "Does this mean he's not going to
turn you in?" I asked Ali.

"He wants to bring his older son to learn about the
Bible and how to become a Christian. He said, 'Make
him just like Tahir! '"

All the air went out of my lungs. Vividly, I recalled the
night of Tahir's conversion. Tahir had asked for a
Christian name. "I will call you Andrew Tahir," Ali
had said, and Dr. Bruckner immediately added, "And
Andrew brought his brother" (see John 1:41). These
words had been prophetic.

Christ meets us where we are. Even though my husband has faith the size of Mt. Everest, the Lord still
held Miss Mustard Seed in His hand that night.

The repressive situation in this country intensified not
long after Judy wrote that account, forcing this couple to escape at night out the back door of their apartment while the
secret police waited for them at the front door. They fled over-

land during the night to another country in the Middle East, where they continue to minister to Muslims, always looking to build relationships with the goal of planting a church.

Another unreached people group in the Middle East is the Druze. Their religion is a mixture of Islam, Judaism, and Christianity. They believe in one God who cannot be understood. Our team in Lebanon is ministering among the 400,000 Druze people. What a privilege to tell them about a God who sent His only Son—Christ, the Messiah—so that we can both know Him and love Him!

A few years ago, there were only two known believers among the Druze. Our team has seen a tremendous breakthrough in Lebanon, where 100 Druze have come to Christ in recent years, and many more have expressed openness to the Gospel! There is a newly established Druze church, and members are actively reaching out to friends, family, and neighbors. One worker shared this amazing report of God's faithfulness:

S is a sixteen-year-old who has been coming faithfully to all our meetings. He also plays percussion (the dirbakkeh) during our worship time. He has been a believer for over a year now.

In January 1999, his brother, N, woke up in the night nauseated and vomiting blood. They rushed him to the hospital and found that he had a bleeding ulcer in his stomach, caused by a very strong antibiotic he was taking to treat a kidney infection. N was at the hospital for six days, during which time he received seven units of blood. Through S, his mother and father asked us to come pray for him at the hospital. Three local believers and I visited him. He was in a two-bed room, and the other patient was a Maronite Christian[9] who also had two guests visiting him. N's mom, dad, and uncle were there, too. We visited for a few minutes, and then asked N if he wanted Jesus to heal him.

He said, "Yes, please, Jesus, heal me."

We prayed for him with our thick accents, and the Maronites in the room were staring, not believing what they were seeing.

The next day, his father came to thank us and told us that N had stopped bleeding and was going in for an endoscopy later that morning. A few days later we heard what happened during the endoscopy. N, who was under local anesthesia, heard the doctor shout in unbelief. He called seven or eight other doctors to come and watch what was happening on the screen. It was the ulcer "zipping up" and healing right before their eyes! The doctors were stunned, saying, "This is from God. It can only be God."

We have had a few Bible studies with N's parents. N is now attending all our meetings with his brother, S. We are pretty certain that N's father and brother have become believers.

Another family from a remote town has also come to faith. The father is a sheik in his sixties, and his son is also a sheik. I am amazed at what God is doing. Who would have thought that a Druze sheik and his family would come to faith in Christ? It is the Lord's doing. What rest and peace we have in the knowledge that He is doing the work. We don't have to keep up the pressure to produce. It is in His hands.

These exciting stories of God's faithfulness are being re-peated all over the world in places such as Kuwait, Turkey, India, Uzbekistan, Hungary, Russia, Vietnam, and unreached areas of Bolivia and Peru. We pray for unreached peoples, and ask God—the Lord of the harvest—to raise up missionary la-borers to go. He answers that prayer and sends them our way. They start or join teams that plant churches. And God con-tinues to work miracles.

These victories often come with a high cost, as the enemy contests ground we have won. We've experienced the joys of seeing God's church grow, and we've also shed tears of grief as we've seen families pay the ultimate price for the Gospel.

Tom and Diane Lawrence, from Houston Chinese Church in Texas, came to PIONEERS in 1984 with a burden for the un-reached people of China. They already had a fruitful ministry to international students from mainland China who were studying at universities in Houston.

Tom and Diane were a natural "fit" for our very first opening in China. At that time, the government of China re-quired that English teachers have doctorate degrees, which Tom did. He and Diane accepted a position in January 1985 teaching English in a remote northeast city in China. They were among the first English teachers to go to China. Today, China environmental standards are far from healthy, but in the days when the Lawrences lived there, the situation was even worse. Most cities in China are heated with coal in the winter, and for many months, it is virtually impossible to see the sky through the black haze of smoke.

Tom was eventually diagnosed with cancer, and he and Diane fought a valiant battle. Tom wrote in a prayer letter to their supporters:

During those days [while teaching in China], I experienced malnutrition for an extended time. I would acquire congestion in my lungs, which I found I had to leave China periodically to recover from, and I frequently found myself in situations where I was breathing dense and unfiltered second-hand tobacco smoke. Under those conditions, it is probable that carcinogenic substances made a home in the congestion in my lung while my immune system was unable to fight back due to the malnutrition.

On July 13, 1993, Tom went home to be with His Lord whom He served so faithfully. He was forty-nine years old. Just before he died, he wrote his supporters:

It was right for us to share Christ with the young people in China, despite the cost. Many of our friends are and will pray for my complete healing. We welcome those prayers, and we are pursuing our lives with that hope in our hearts. However, we want to clarify that our faith does not hinge on God's willingness to heal, but on Christ's victory over death. We believe that we will be raised up together to share in Christ's glory at the resurrection of New Testament believers toward the end of this age.

Tom was not the only one who would remind us of that. Henry Kim, his wife, Mi-Suk, and their three young children were so enthusiastic about their ministry to the unreached that they left for the field just six weeks after going through PIONEERS candidate orientation.

Henry was born in Korea, and in 1988 emigrated to the United States where he earned masters degrees in divinity and missions/intercultural studies. When he and his family joined one of our teams in Central Asia, they were a valuable addition and looked forward to many years of service to the unreached. But after just eight months, they were forced to return to the U.S. because of Henry's declining health. Their plan was for Henry to receive the necessary medical attention, and after a period of rest, return to the field. Henry was diagnosed with colon cancer, however, and underwent what the family thought was successful surgery. While Henry received chemotherapy, he and his family remained in the Chicago area where their home church, Korean Bethel Presbyterian, cared for them.

"I am beginning to realize that a missionary not in a mission field is like a fish away from water," Henry wrote while in the U.S. "Central Asia was a place where I can experience freedom as a missionary. However, I believe that there must be a purpose why God has allowed me to stay here in Chicago. I am in Chicago. However, God, who is in Central Asia, will answer our prayers and continue His work there."

It was Henry's sincere desire to return "home" to the field to be in the place where God had called him, but in the Father's sovereign plan, Henry was called to his Heavenly home. He was just thirty-three years old.

Like the Lawrences, Henry and Mi-Suk served in a part of the world with harmful environmental exposure—in their case an area where hazardous, and possibly nuclear, wastes were probably dumped by the former Soviet Union. A number of missionaries working in the same area also developed cancer around the same time that Henry did. We take comfort in the words from Psalm 116:15: "Precious in the sight of the Lord is the death of his saints" (NIV).

Not every missionary pays with his or her life, but the costs can still be extremely high. PIONEERS workers in resistant countries are not immune from the persecution that the local

Christians endure, of course. The situation in Indonesia has been extremely dangerous for Christians in the past few years. In certain volatile areas, churches have been burned to the ground, Christian women and girls have been raped, and many believers have been brutally murdered. Our national co-workers have paid dearly for the sake of the Gospel, including Pastor Seth and his family, who opened their home to a Muslim high school student interested in Christianity. The girl feared that her own family would put her in stocks if they found out about her questions—a typical treatment for people considered to be mentally unstable (including Muslim converts to Christianity). Pastor Seth was arrested and charged with abducting a minor, forced conversion, and rape. Although there was no evidence to support the charges, of course, the community brought the case to trial, and Pastor Seth received a ten-year sentence. Two other pastors, their wives, and the church secretary were sentenced to six years each.

The situation in Indonesia has also affected PIONEERS missionaries. One of our families serving there was brutally attacked during a robbery in their home. The husband was stabbed three times, puncturing his lung and missing his heart by less than a centimeter. The entire family, including the two children who witnessed the attack, still have deep emotional scars. We'll never know if this brave family was targeted for persecution because of their faith, or if they were robbed because they were foreigners.

One of our single missionaries in Kazakhstan miraculously escaped harm when two men forced their way into her apartment and violently beat her and her roommate. She later wrote to her supporters:

God continues to astound me with the depth of His

grace. When I returned to my apartment to clean up the blood-splattered walls, floors, and cabinets, I thought of the cross. When we think of Christ dying, we have a very sanitary picture of a little blood dripping neatly down His head onto the ground. But the cross was violent, ruthless, cruel. Jesus' blood was splattered all over Jerusalem. He knew we would beat Him and kill Him, and He came anyway. That's how much He loved us. That's how much He loved me. That's how much He loved the men who attacked me. That's how big He is.

After such a traumatic experience, no one would have blamed this missionary for giving up and returning to the U.S. But she desired to stay, and she and her roommate even moved back into their apartment and are being used by God to reach out to those around them.

Like Paul, we know that our struggle is not against flesh and blood, but against spiritual forces of evil (see Ephesians 6:12). When our teams disrupt the centuries-old strongholds of evil, anything can happen. One of our summer teams in Sumatra, for example, prayed on top of Mount Merapi, the center of many regional superstitions and legends. The team asked God to bind evil, release his Spirit, and flood the villages with the knowledge of the glory of the Lord. On the way down the mountain, just as the team was crossing its volcanic crater and passing a few feet from the central gaping hole, the mountain exploded. It was the biggest eruption since 1976, and a town ten miles away was blanketed with ash half an inch deep. The sky turned so black that headlights and street lights were needed at midday. Miraculously, our team escaped death, although they suffered third-degree burns. Obviously their prayers were right on target; since that time, the number of nationals finding Christ has doubled every year, and the New Testament and the *Jesus* film are now available in the local language.

Our own family has not been immune to paying the price for taking the Gospel to the ends of the earth. Our grandson, Gary Paul Franz, Jr., was born on the mission field in Indonesia with severe hydrocephalus. He was not expected to live more than a few days. His parents—our daughter and son-in-law, Carol and Gary Franz—had to give up their dream to serve as foreign missionaries because Gary Paul needed critical medical attention. After eleven years of brain surgeries and emergencies, Gary Paul is still alive—and still glorifying God through his life. Although he can't talk, Gary Paul can preach—and has preached volumes to us about God's faithfulness, loving care, higher ways, and how He still allows mysteries in our lives that will only be fully understood in Heaven.

There are many other PIONEERS workers whom I could mention who have paid high prices for the privilege of serving their King. But even if they had known when they started how high the cost would be, I doubt they would have turned back. The very nature of being a pioneer means leaving the safe harbor and going into uncharted territory, which can be full of hazards—some even life threatening. When PIONEERS began, we knew there would be some workers who would lose their lives for the sake of the Gospel. Our missionaries are all aware of this when they leave for the field and are prepared to pay the ultimate price, believing without hesitation that the harvest is worth the cost.

We'll never know why the Lord chooses to take someone like Tom Lawrence (an experienced missionary) or Henry Kim (young and ready to take on the world). "God is God," said Elisabeth Elliott following the martyrdom of her husband, Jim, when they were missionaries to the unreached Auca tribe

God Called a Family

With our children and grandchildren, 1998

Our grandson, Gary Paul Franz, Jr., age 11

With siblings (Back row, left to right: John, Waller [now with the Lord], Ted, Bill, Harry. Seated left to right: Mary Jane and Martha)

in the jungles of Ecuador. She realized that we cannot explain God's moves in nice, pat terms. He can do as He chooses. Even our attempt to provide a reason for martyrdom—such as the well-known quote, "The blood of the martyrs is the seed of the Church"—is simply our need to explain God's actions. He certainly doesn't need us to do that.

Tom and Henry will probably not be the last PIONEERS missionaries to give their lives for the Gospel. Nor will the other workers I've shared about here be the only ones to endure heart-breaking and seemingly inexplicable suffering.

Thankfully, we have this unshakeable promise to hold on to: "Those who sow in tears will reap with songs of joy. He who goes out weeping, carrying seed to sow, will return with songs of joy, carrying sheaves with him" (Psalm 126:5-6 NIV).

The devil does not have the final say—in this nor any matter. Our God is the Alpha and the Omega, the first and the last, and He always has the last word. As Tom Lawrence wrote just before he died, our faith lies in the fact that Jesus has given us the ultimate victory over death.

I have fought the good fight, I have finished the race, I have kept the faith. Now there is in store for me the crown of righteousness, which the Lord, the righteous Judge, will award to me on that day—and not only to me, but also to all who have longed for his appearing (2 Timothy 4:7-8 NIV).

CHAPTER 10

From All Nations

There before me was a great multitude that no one could count, from every nation, tribe, people and language, standing before the throne and in front of the Lamb.

—Revelation 7:9 (NIV)

Missions is no longer the "West to the rest" but is now "everywhere to everywhere."

—Nate Wilson

What a sight! I looked around the room and felt as if I were at the United Nations with people to my right and left from many nations, languages, and tribes. This wasn't a U.N. meeting, however. It was the PIONEERS International Summit, and the men and women at the table were leaders of emerging PIONEERS bases all over the world—Africa, Australia, Canada, Europe, New Zealand, Singapore, and the United States.

That historic meeting was held in Chicago in September 1997. It was an amazing moment to realize that in just eighteen years the Lord had expanded our "tent pegs" from one family working around their dining room table to an international body of believers strategizing around a board room table.

From our early days as a mission, God gave us the vision to reach the unreached wherever they are. We continually reminded ourselves that God didn't say, "Go into all the world where you can get a missionary visa." He just said, "Go into all the world."

"To all the world" has certainly been our call. But there was another call as well: "from all the world." We didn't want PIONEERS to be just a U.S.-based ministry. To reach the entire world effectively, we had to represent the entire world—to find workers who were *from* all the world and send them *to* all the world. We felt it would honor our Lord if our missionaries came from many different countries, cultures, and backgrounds—to reach the unreached within their own borders, and to join international teams going to other parts of the world.

That foundational belief led us to a process we call "internationalization," as we worked to make PIONEERS as international as possible. It didn't happen overnight. We started small and grew through relationships that God sovereignly gave us. By His grace, today we have mobilization bases in Africa, Australia, Canada, Europe, New Zealand, Singapore, and the U.S. Each base focuses on recruiting laborers from their countries to join PIONEERS teams all over the world.

PIONEERS-Africa is a good example of this process of internationalization. Although this mobilization base is now sending Africans all over the continent and eventually the world, you could say that it all started under a tree. That's where Dr. Solomon Aryeetey, director of PIONEERS-Africa, used to conduct his medical clinics—under a tree in front of his house in the desert of Mali, West Africa.

Solomon grew up in Ghana as the son of a polygamist who had five wives. His mother was the fourth wife, and Solomon likes to say, "If my dad were not a polygamist, I would not have been born, and that would have been very sad

for the world!" His family lived in harsh, poverty-stricken conditions, but Solomon was determined to become a doctor and
pull himself out of poverty. He accepted Christ as a teenager.
When he graduated from medical school in 1979, he made
plans to move to the United States so that he could, in his
words, make "big bucks." God had other plans for him.

In 1986, when Solomon was getting ready to settle in the
U.S., a PIONEERS representative challenged him to use his
medical skills in a new outreach to the Muslim Fulani people
of Mali, West Africa. He and his wife, Letitia, an attorney,
sensed the invitation was from God. They gave up their prac-
tices, joined PIONEERS, bought a four-wheel drive vehicle, and
moved to the desert in Mali, 700 miles away from their home.
When they weren't holding medical clinics under the tree in
their front yard, they'd drive into the desert and look for nomadic groups of Fulani. During the day, they would treat
physical needs with medicine, and during the evening, they
would minister to the Fulani's spiritual needs by sharing the
Gospel and showing the *Jesus* film. For the first eighteen
months, Solomon and Letitia had only a few converts to show
for all their labor, but they kept on working for the Lord.
Then something extraordinary happened, which I'll let
Solomon tell in his own words:

> When we went to visit our Fulani friends and converts
> one evening, their leader called us into a meeting. He
> explained that he and his elders had had a meeting the
> previous day to discuss what they were going to do
> with us and our ministry among them. They were
> eager to hear my answer to a very important question
> before they made up their mind. "Are you loving us
> the way you do and showing us all this kindness
> purely out of love because of your Book from which
> you have been reading to us? We give you nothing for

all your services. You help evacuate our sick to the hospital. You give us transportation freely. You take care of our sick women and children. Are you this way because of your Book?"

When I answered, "Yes," this is what they replied: "In that case, we too want the message of your Book! From now on, you are one of us. You are free to come among us and show our people the ways of Isa [Jesus]!"

From that day on, I wondered what we were going to do with such a wide open door! The more I prayed to the Lord about more laborers, the more He convinced me that it was time for more Africans to get involved with reaching the lost on our continent for Christ.

Solomon and Letitia spent the next nine years reaching the nomadic Fulani for Christ. Two churches were planted, and local leaders carry on the work to this day.

While their children were young, they lived with relatives in Ghana, but as the children got older and needed more of their parents' attention, Solomon and Letitia sought the Lord on what to do. The Lord was fine-tuning the "bigger picture" vision that He had given them for all of Africa: They had the potential to do much more for world evangelism than they were currently doing, particularly raising up other missionaries like themselves.

One night in 1992 while the couple was on a ministry trip to the U.S., the Lord put a strong message on Solomon's heart. It was so compelling that he woke up Letitia and told her to write down what the Lord was saying to him: "The Lord is telling me that tomorrow, when the two of us go to

Orlando, John Fletcher is going to call us into his office and share something important with us. This is going to confirm to us that it is God's new direction, and we should say yes to John."

So the next day as they sat in John's office, Solomon and Letitia were prepared to hear from God. John asked them a simple question: "Is it possible for you to start a mission to send more African missionaries like you to the field?" That's all Solomon needed to hear because he had the very same idea. Solomon had his marching orders, and he and Letitia eventually moved from Mali back to Ghana, where they established PIONEERS-Africa, with Solomon as director.

What began as a small enterprise of two missionaries among the Fulani in Mali has rapidly grown to involve four African countries with PIONEERS directors and boards in Ghana, Mali, Benin, and Togo. Each raises up Christian workers within those countries to evangelize not only on PIONEERS teams in Africa, but eventually on teams in other parts of the world. Today PIONEERS-Africa numbers more than 100 missionaries, with the potential for many more. Solomon says there is a growing awareness in the African church that the remaining task of evangelization of their continent is primarily their responsibility. He describes the potential as a "volcano that is begging to explode."

The stories of the wonderful move of the Lord through PIONEERS-Africa can also be told about our mobilization bases in other parts of the world. PIONEERS-Canada, for example, which was born from a merger in 1994 between PIONEERS and World Outreach Fellowship, opened up our first fields in Latin America. Teams are now touching unreached fishermen in coastal Brazil and preparing to reach the Mascho of Peru. Radio broadcasts jointly sponsored by PIONEERS and other mission agencies reach 2-3 million Quechua in Bolivia living in villages and towns in some of the most inaccessible terrain imaginable.

In India, hundreds of churches have been planted through the ministry of Sam and Rachel Paulson and more than 150 Indian evangelists associated with PIONEERS-India. PIONEERS-Europe has a thriving ministry among the unreached peoples of former Soviet satellites. PIONEERS of Australia and PIONEERS-New Zealand (formed as a result of mergers between South Sea Evangelical Mission and Asia Pacific Christian Mission) opened new harvest fields for us in Irian Jaya, Fiji, Cambodia, and the Solomon Islands. PIONEERS-Singapore, one of our newest bases, is part of a move of God in this tiny city-state, which many have called the "Antioch of Asia," referring to the Antioch church in the Book of Acts that had a heart for missions and the harvest. And we recently launched a new mobilization office in Brazil. Over the next twenty-five years, mission experts believe that Brazil will emerge as one of the strongest missionary-sending countries in world evangelization.

PIONEERS-USA is a mobilization base, and also serves as the hub of the global operations of PIONEERS-USA. The Orlando Team now numbers fifty-four—a far cry from the small volunteer staff we began with back in 1979. When I served in Korea, I knew that for every Marine on the frontlines, ten others backed them up. For PIONEERS, the reverse is true: For every ten missionaries on the frontlines, there is one Orlando Team member behind them.

The Apostle Paul asked, "How, then, can they call on the one they have not believed in? And how can they believe in the one of whom they have not heard? And how can they hear without someone preaching to them? And how can they preach unless they are sent?" (Romans 10:14-15 NIV). Paul knew that the starting point to reach the lost is sending missionaries to the unreached. In order to have go-ers, there must be senders, and that is the role of the Orlando Team: to partner with churches to mobilize, prepare, and support missionaries among unreached peoples. As we began the process of internationalization, there was still one missing piece. We needed a structure that would provide servant-leadership to all the PIONEERS bases. In February 1998, the U.S. board authorized formation of an International Council to provide oversight and accountability worldwide.

A month later, the Council held its first meeting in Auckland, New Zealand, embracing the new global structure of the mission and appointing PIONEERS first international director, Dr. C. Douglas McConnell. We first met Doug back in the 1980s when he was a missionary to Papua New Guinea serving with Asia Pacific Christian Mission (APCM) and in partnership with our team. Doug later became APCM's general director and then chair of the Department of Missions/Intercultural Studies and Evangelism at Wheaton Graduate School in Illinois. He also served as chair of our U.S. board, so it was a natural fit to see him become our international director. Doug leads our international coordinating team, which includes John Fain, our director of international ministries, and Donnie Scearce, our international mobilization coordinator.

Like our friendship with Doug, many of the countries now represented around the PIONEERS table go back to relationships formed years earlier. Some were missionaries whom Peggy and I supported four decades ago; others were young students from Bible colleges, or national leaders we first met at conferences. These people and many others like them were the key players in the growth of PIONEERS, and we're so grateful that the Lord brought us together with them. They helped us to expand our borders and reach many more needy people around the world. "He gave them the lands of the nations, and they fell heir to what others had toiled for" (Psalm 105:44 NIV).

CHAPTER 11

A New Era

I consider my life worth nothing to me, if only I may finish the race and complete the task the Lord Jesus has given me—the task of testifying to the gospel of God's grace.

—Acts 20:24 (NIV)

If it be possible, let us try to set some work going that will glorify Him when we are dead and gone. Let us scatter some seed that may spring up when we are sleeping beneath the hillock in the cemetery.

—Charles H. Spurgeon

A few years after my father passed away in 1964, I visited his old Kentucky home. When I knocked on the door of the neighbors' house, the first thing they said to me was, "Orville Fletcher's eyes." Without knowing exactly who I was, they remembered my father's eyes and saw those same eyes in me.

I don't know if I ever resembled Dad that much outwardly, but as his namesake son, I was destined to carry his name through life. For me, it wasn't his eyes that captivated me as much as his heart. I longed to be like Dad inwardly, a man of strong character. Yet at times Dad seemed to be everything that I was not and everything I wanted to be. I was the ordinary son of a great father and a great mother who raised five sons and two daughters. In their steps I would follow, but I was certain I would never be as great as they were.

Many years later, Peggy and I spent Christmas in Indonesia with our daughter, Ginny, and her husband, Ken Mauger. By this time, they had already been in Indonesia several years, following a term in South Africa working among Hindus and Muslims. Their eldest son, Kenny, who was just a youngster at the time, asked me one of those direct questions that only kids are bold enough to ask: "Grandpa, am I going to get an inheritance someday?"

I chuckled, and shared with him about the riches that we have in Christ—one of the many lessons I had learned long ago from my father. The morning I had that talk with Kenny, I came across Proverbs 13:22 in my quiet time with the Lord: "A good man leaves an inheritance for his children's children" (NIV).

But what inheritance do Peggy and I have to pass on to our children and our children's children? I wondered. We certainly don't have much in terms of material possessions or dollars and cents. But our parents didn't either. Beyond earthly treasures is something of far greater significance and worth: the lasting treasure of a ministry to unreached peoples, "treasures in heaven, where moth and rust do not destroy, and where thieves do not break in and steal" (Matthew 6:20 NIV).

What an inheritance to leave for the next generation!

I'm so grateful to the Lord that He came calling in four generations of our family. Today, our four children and their spouses are all in full-time missions work. Many of our grandchildren were born on the field—in countries that Peggy and I prayed for decades ago. Just as God gave our family a heart for the unreached, He faithfully linked us with like-minded people all over the globe.

Today, at the dawn of the third millennium, the international family of PIONEERS works in nearly fifty countries—approximately eighty-five ministry teams, several hundred national workers, and more than 800 international members (missionaries, staff, and board). In all, these dedicated workers share God's love with more than 100 unreached people groups in some of the most remote places on the planet.

With the psalmist, we can truly say, "The Lord has done this, and it is marvelous in our eyes" (Psalm 118:23 NIV).

In early 1999, our son, John, concluded it was time to step down as executive director. During his ten and one-half years in office, he did a foundational work in taking the mission from infancy to maturity—something I could not have done. John wanted to stay involved with the mission, but felt that God had another role for him, and another person to serve as president. He now serves as director of global partnerships for PIONEERS-USA. Peggy and I work with him, along with Will and Nancy Chandler, to help represent and raise support for national ministries and evangelist/church-planters among the unreached—an important part of the original vision of PIONEERS. Hundreds of these nationals are already at work with us, and thousands more can be mobilized.

When John stepped down, the board appointed Steve Richardson to take his place as president of the U.S. operations of PIONEERS. Steve had already served with us for eight years as team leader, and five years as area director for Island Southeast Asia and Oceania, supervising fifteen of our missionary teams. The board knew he was a gifted man, still in his thirties yet with a proven track record of leadership on the field, and dedicated to the Lord as well as to the vision and values of PIONEERS.

When Steve was a boy growing up in the jungles of Irian Jaya, he remembers spending time with his father under the stars at night. His dad would point out various constellations and talk about God's promise to Abraham 4,000 years earlier—that all nations would be blessed through him and that his descendants would be as numerous as the stars. Steve was impressed by the impact of the Gospel on the tribal people around him, by his parents' faith, and by God's redemptive plan in the Scriptures, and he determined that he, too, wanted to be a blessing to the world. Throughout his youth and college years, he unwaveringly pursued this missionary call.

God's promise to Abraham—His redemptive plan for the nations—is a two-fold promise: "I will bless you" and "All peoples on earth will be blessed through you" (Genesis 12:1, 3 NIV). You and I are the ones whom God has called to take Abraham's blessing to the world. We are in the midst of an incredible era of need, but also an incredible era of harvest. Many people lament the fact that the "dark is getting darker"—and it is:

- 15 million children die every year from preventable diseases.
- 1 billion people don't have access to basic health care, education, drinking water, or nutrition.
- Eighty percent of the world's youth grow up in non-Christian homes.
- The number of refugees has exploded from 3 million in 1970 to more than 25 million today. [10]

Yes, the dark *is* getting darker, but thanks be to our God, the light is also getting brighter. In twenty years, evangelical Christians have quadrupled in number—from 150 million to 560 million.[11] That's nearly ten percent of the world's population.

The Bible promises, "Nations will come to your light, and kings to the brightness of your dawn" (Isaiah 60:3 NIV). As I look at the miracles God has worked during PIONEERS first two decades, I am excited to anticipate what He's going to do in the future. The next twenty years—if the Lord should tarry that long—will prove to be an even greater chronicle of His working with us and through us. I am convinced we are on the edge of an unbelievable era of harvest such as the world has never before seen.

Led by a Straight Way

To prepare for this harvest, the Lord led us to move our headquarters about a decade ago from outside Washington, D.C., to Orlando, Florida. We were blessed by our time in Washington, particularly by our close relationship with Faith Bible Church (FBC) in Sterling, Virginia, which was a lifeline to us. The church has been with us since the very founding of the ministry, and over the years has given more than $1 million in support for PIONEERS missionaries and projects—an astounding figure for a local church. In addition, FBC has sent countless missionaries our way, and served as a constant source of wisdom, direction, and counsel.

As much as we valued our location in Washington, it was clear financially that we had to make a move. The cost of living in the capital area is high. In order to expand our reach overseas, we needed land where our home ministry base could grow, which would be difficult in the Washington area because of cost and availability of land and office space.

The Lord gave us Psalm 107:7 as both direction and a promise: "He led them by a straight way to a city where they could settle" (NIV). After surveying more than 100 possible sites, we purchased forty acres of land in southeast Orlando on the shores of Lake Whippoorwill. One of the unique features of the property is that it includes a KOA Campground, which helps us financially, because we operate it as a separate for-profit business, and also helps us practically, because we own some trailers on site that provide a place for a few of our staff and visiting missionaries to stay.

Our relocation to Orlando has enabled us to grow and expand. In 1996, we launched a $3.5 million campaign to raise funds for the first phase of our facilities, which were dedicated in February 1999. The efficiently designed Missionary Service Center, with its striking Prayer Tower, replaces the two mobile trailer units where our staff worked for four years. These new facilities help us better serve our missionaries and those they reach.

PIONEERS-USA Headquarters, Orlando, Florida

Orlando Team

Our next phase of development, called "Bridge To The World," will help us achieve our strategic goal of doubling our U.S. missionary force within the next five years. We see these new facilities as "bridge-building tools." A Missionary Training Center will equip more than 100 U.S. missionaries each year, provide others with short-term housing, and care for missionaries and their families as needs arise. Additional offices in a new Global Ministry Center will enable us to help individuals and churches all over the U.S. get involved in ministry to unreached peoples.

Blazing New Paths

For PIONEERS to be true to its name and heritage, wherever we are in our history should always be just the beginning—the beginning to:

- Challenge new frontiers
- Seek new impossibilities
- Undertake giant ventures for God
- Discover and penetrate new unreached people groups with the message of Christ's love

I'm grateful that God opened my eyes to see that the most significant thing happening in the world is not taking place in the U.S. military or on Wall Street. It is God's program of world evangelization. It is a continuation of Genesis chapter 12 when He set in motion a vast plan to redeem the world back to Himself.

The history of PIONEERS is really "His-story"—God's story. He happened to use people who were ordinary Christians willing to be His vessels—thousands of PIONEERS missionaries, staff, leaders, supporters, intercessors, and volunteers around the world. Each of us started with a dream, something God called us to do that seemed absolutely impossible.

When God came calling in my life, I knew I wanted to be a part of a movement that was stamped by a sense of destiny. I still want nothing less. My passion is to see the Lord of the harvest raise up a body of men and women who are an elite force, risking all and willing to die to take Christ where He is not known.

Jesus commenced this extraordinary work when He came calling on a group of fishermen—ordinary people with normal, everyday lives. "Follow Me," He said to them, "and I will make you fishers of men" (see Matthew 4:19). He gave them a dream to be pioneers.

What about you? Do you sense that God has come calling in your own life? What pioneering dream has He given you to help get the task done? Maybe you don't feel worthy or trained or adequate for the job. Neither did I! God uses all kinds of people. What a thrill it is to see people offer themselves to God as broken, empty vessels, and watch Him use them to play a significant role in world evangelization.

When God came calling on Peggy and me, it was a lot like those tall ships I once saw gracing New York's harbor. We left the safe port to sail on unknown seas, not really knowing where God would take us. But in obedience, we went, trusting Him to bless us, and through us to "bless all the peoples of the earth."

What an adventure it has been! You can be a part of that adventure, too. God has given you special gifts, skills, and interests that He gave to no one else on the planet. Has He also given you a vision for the unreached? You can be a vital part of the final era of world evangelization, either by going yourself, or by mobilizing, sending, praying, or giving.

The growth of Christianity in the past two decades has been nothing short of miraculous. Yet, an astonishing two billion people remain unreached.

A young man on a college campus once asked me, "Why are the Muslims making such progress in Africa?"

"Because you're sitting here," I replied.

God has given us open doors, and we need to move through them as fast as we can. I encourage you to step outside what is known and comfortable, to press ahead in spite of objections, to think outside the box and off the beaten path. If you can't see very far ahead, go ahead as far as you can see. This is the time to leave the harbor, to be a pioneer. Somewhere a life is waiting to be touched and changed—in the mountains of Bolivia, inside a Bedouin tent in Egypt, in a bamboo hut in Papua New Guinea, or within the walls of an English-language class in China. It can happen through you or someone like you.

Jesus gave us a word of warning: "As long as it is day, we must do the work of him who sent me. Night is coming, when no one can work" (John 9:4 NIV).

Today we have an unprecedented—and urgent—opportunity to work while it is still day. "Closed doors" mean nothing to the Lord. In country after country, God has given access to the people who are on His heart. How will we respond? Will we go through the doors that He has opened before us?

"Rescue the perishing; don't hesitate to step in and help. If you say, 'Hey, that's none of my business,' will that get you off the hook?" (Proverbs 24:12, TMB).

You and I must live with the end in mind, that one day we will meet the Father and give an answer for how we responded to Him when He came calling in our lives. My goal is to please Him and hear Him say, "Well done, good and faithful servant! ...Come and share your master's happiness!" (Matthew 25:21 NIV).

As I look to the future, I pray that our greatest years—and yours—are ahead:

- that our trust will remain in God alone
- that our vision will remain clear
- that our zeal will be as strong as in the days of our youth and that we will not lose the boldness to choose the road less traveled, to blaze new paths, and to risk great things for God.

On a recent trip to Egypt, I traveled overland across the desert of the Sinai Peninsula with a PIONEERS missionary as my guide. The long day ended with a midnight swim in the Red Sea, not far from our team's base of ministry to the Bedouins. I rejoiced that our workers have already blazed a path enabling them to reach these Muslim nomads. Yet just across the Gulf of Aqaba, I could see the lights of Saudi Arabia twinkling a mere eleven miles away. The distance is not far physically, but spiritually a chasm exists that makes Saudi Arabia one of the least evangelized countries on earth. No Christian workers are permitted, all Christian literature is banned, and Saudis who confess Christ face death if discovered.

What will it take to reach Saudi Arabia for Christ? What will it take to see Saudi Arabians—and Kurds and Fulani and Sundanese—worshiping around the throne of God someday, bowing not toward a dead god or a merciless prophet, but to the holy and righteous King of kings?

It will take a generation of international pioneers—bold men and women who hear the footsteps of God when He comes calling in their lives, who hear Him asking, "Will you go where no one has gone before? Will you help send the Gospel to the ends of the earth?" I trust you will be ready to answer His call.

What will it take to reach Saudi Arabians —and others who have no opportunity to hear— with the saving knowledge of Jesus Christ?

ENDNOTES

[1] Excerpted from *I Saw Your Sons at War: The Korean Diary of Billy Graham,* copyright 1953 by The Billy Graham Evangelistic Association. Used by permission. All rights reserved.

[2] Now Columbia International University.

[3] A sixth block—secular—was later added.

[4] At the time, missiologists estimated there were as many as 17,000 ethnic groups around the world without a meaningful Gospel witness. There was no clearinghouse of information back then, and later on when research was done, the statistics became more accurate. Today experts estimate there are more than 1,500 ethnic groups that are still unreached, representing two to three billion people. Even those figures are uncertain because researchers use different criteria to define "unreached." The bottom line is that there are many people who still need to hear, and we must be very intentional and proactive to get the job done. The task of fulfilling the Great Commission is far from complete.

[5] One of the children that our family had sponsored twenty years earlier through World Vision was a Sundanese girl. At the time, of course, we had no idea that our own daughters would one day go to the Sundanese as missionaries. Who knew what God was doing through our prayers thirty years earlier for a child who was part of one of the largest unreached people groups in the world?

[6] *Juche: A Christian Study of North Korea's State Religion,* by Thomas J. Belke, Living Sacrifice Book Company, 1999.

[7] *The New Context of World Mission,* by Bryant L. Myers, Mission Advanced Research and Communications Center, a division of World Vision International, 1996.

[8] Another PIONEERS team, focusing on Albanians, was based in Macedonia and helped extensively with the refugee crisis as it spilled into Macedonia. Growing out of this is a team now based in Kosovo.

[9] Arabic-speaking Christians. In the nineteenth century, many Maronites were massacred by the Druze.

[10] *The New Context of World Mission,* by Bryant L. Myers, Mission Advanced Research and Communications Center, a division of World Vision International, 1996.

[11] *Advance,* October 1995.

How to Contact PIONEERS

On the web: www.pioneers.org

In the U.S.:

PIONEERS–USA
12343 Narcoossee Road
Orlando, FL 32827
(800) 755-7284 telephone
(407) 382-6000 telephone
(407) 382-1008 fax
usa@pioneers.org

International Offices:

PIONEERS–Africa
P.O. Box CT 394
Cantonments, Accra
Ghana, West Africa
233-21-50-20-77 telephone
piafrica@africaonline.com.gh

PIONEERS of Australia
4/46 New Street, Suite 4
Ringwood
Victoria 3134
Australia
61-3-9879-2900 telephone
info@pioneers.org.au

PIONEERS in Brazil
Rua UB 31/55 Cond. Altos da Serra II - Urbanova
São José dos Campos, SP - 12244-511 Brazil
(55) 012-39492251 telephone/fax

PIONEERS–Canada
51 Byron Avenue
Dorchester, ON N0L 1G2
Canada
(519) 268-8778 telephone
Canada@PIONEERS.org

PIONEERS–Europe
Jozsef Attila ut. 25
2049 Diosd
Budapest, Hungary
36-23-374-101 telephone
40_80_window@compuserve.com

PIONEERS–New Zealand
35 Karaka Street
P.O. Box 68 376
Newton, Auckland 1
New Zealand
64-9-377-2455 telephone
admin@mobilising.co.nz

PIONEERS In Asia (Singapore) Ltd.
Orchard P.O.
P.O. Box 670
Singapore 912323
65-732-7181 fax

WANT MORE INFORMATION?

Please send me more information about:

☐ Becoming a missionary with PIONEERS

☐ Involving my local church in missions

☐ Praying for PIONEERS missionaries

☐ Giving financially to the work of PIONEERS

☐ The Edge summer teams

PLEASE PRINT:

Name_____

Address_____

City _____

State _____ ZIP _____

Country_____

Telephone_____

Email_____

Mail this page to any of the PIONEERS mobilization bases listed on the previous pages.